I Know All About You!

The True Power of Astropsychology

Louis Turi, M.D.S.

Visit Dr. Turi on the World Wide Web at
http://www.drturi.com

E-mail to: Dr.Turi@juno.com

I Know All About You!

The True Power of Astropsychology

Louis Turi, M.D.S.

Copyright © 2004 by Re-evolution Press
Copyright © 2004 by Dr. Louis Turi

All rights reserved. No part of this publication may be reproduced or transmitted in any form or by any means, electronic or mechanical, including photocopying, recording, or any information storage and retrieval system, without permission in writing from the publisher.

Cover art by Chris Tittle
and Madeline Rosenstein
www.madroseart.com

Book design and typography by
David Sielaff and Nancy Melton of San Diego

ISBN 0-966731-24-7

Re-evolution Press
19633 Ventura Blvd., Suite B
Tarzana, Ca. 91356

www.reevolutionpress.com
http://www.truthseekersnetwork.com

Visit Dr. Turi on the web at:
www.drturi.com

Printed in the United States of America

Table of Contents

Introduction
Important Note From Dr. Turi
Sun Sign Characteristics For Those Born In:
    April 1
    May 3
    June 5
    July 7
    August 9
    September 11
    October 13
    November 15
    December 17
    January 19
    February 21
    March 23
Explanation Of The Housing System 25
Astropsychology Profile:
    Aries 29
    Taurus 44
    Gemini 60
    Cancer 77
    Leo 93
    Virgo 109
    Libra 124
    Scorpio 138
    Sagittarius 153
    Capricorn 169
    Aquarius 185
    Pisces 200

Responses From My Readers 216
Closing Thoughts 220
About the Illustrator 222
Startheme Ltd. 223
Astropsychology — Products to Order 224
Astrological Services — Courses 227
Order Form 232-4
Order Form 235-6
Front Cover Illustrator 297

Acknowledgments

A special thanks to all the spiritual readers from all walks of life. Man's spiritual journey is infinite and starts in the Universal Mind. One must learn and trust in the undeniable laws governing the human spirit.

— Dr. Turi

Introduction

This material will allow you to uncover the secrets of the Universal Mind and know all you need to know about a friend, a lover, a family member and even your own self. Understanding and following this simple technique will allow you to read a person almost immediately and to a great extent, anywhere, anytime with uncanny accuracy. Keep in mind that Nostradamus' rare method of Divine Astrology or Astropsychology is used in this original method. Dr. Turi's style is unique and does not reflect the modern approach of mundane astrology that you may have read, learned or practiced.

This is how we will proceed:
1. Familiarize yourself with the Astro-Psychology Sun Sign Characteristics and read this section a few times.
2. Master the Housing System and understand the twelve specific areas of the human experience.
3. Build up a subconscious reflex by assimilating all the information from the Housing System for each sign of the zodiac.

As pretentious as it may sound, you will know more than any and all psychologists, psychiatrists, so-called psychics and modern astrologers combined together.

"Man is superior to the stars if he lives in the power of superior wisdom. Such a person being the master over heaven and earth, by means of his will, is a magus and magic is not sorcery but supreme wisdom."
— ***Paracelcus***

Important Note from Dr. Turi

Born and raised in Provence, France, I rekindled and only exercise Nostradamus' 16th-Century Divine Astrology method. This formula does not reflect the modern astrology disciplines you may use, study, or practice. Realize that over 500 years ago the famous Prophet did not use a watch or any sophisticated computers. Thus, like the great Seer, I investigate the outer space and the Universal Mind with my inborn spiritual telescope. A "microscopic attitude" will not help anyone to gain the golden key of spiritual knowledge. This limited, exploitative attitude is for "astronomers" who have long lost their cosmic consciousness with their rigid mathematical minds. We have all heard of "not seeing the forest for the trees." Every one of them is aware of the twelve constellations of the Zodiac; somehow it is still impossible for them to pass the limitations of their five rational senses.

To penetrate the intuition, its very domain, and decode the subtle meaning behind each symbol does take more than mere numbers. Realize that Divine Astrology is an extremely old celestial art and a very complex science and must be practiced as such. Not everyone is blessed with the "gift" needed to assimilate, understand, and translate correctly the heavenly dexterity of the Creator. That is why a section of the bible clearly mentions, "I will talk to you, but you won't hear me! I will present myself to you, but you won't see me!" God speaks to us within his own manifestation and through his Divine light only. Only those willing to expand their cosmic consciousness will be able to "perceive and receive." Be curious, be critical, keep an open mind and don't let induced religious fears stop you in gaining a new light. Simply "ask, and you shall receive" the understanding of God's celestial manifestation. For those born on the cusp of any zodiac sign, simply refer to the month of your birth, which reflects the exact constellation of your nativity. Divine Astrology, as practiced by Nostradamus, is the original way at looking at the stars, as did the great Seer. My students have found it to be incredibly accurate!

In all affairs involving the mind and spirit, traditionalists and scientists alike are missing the obvious. Looking down will not bring the answers they are so desperately looking for. It is above and in the Universal Mind that one will find the golden keys to what it means to be human.

— Dr. Turi

Sun Sign Characteristics

Philosophical Astro-Poetry by Brigitte Turi

**Mars Governs the Aggressive Warlike
and Impatient Constellation Of Aries**

*All will hear my views and voice
Trial and error is my school of choice
Like a dragon, dashing and daring I appear
Fighting for those that I hold dear
I am ARIES, child of Mars.*

Characteristics For Those Born In April

Aggressive Mars controls the month of April. This planet traditionally rules the impatient sign of Aries. These souls are born leaders but because of their natural impatience they are also prone to learn by their mistakes. The strong, impatient desire to succeed must be controlled and hasty decisions avoided. They are perceived as the warrior of astrology. More than any other sign of the zodiac, those born in April must learn steadiness, organization, and most of all diplomacy. When confronted, grace and charm does not really belong to them. Martian souls possess strong leadership and engineering abilities, and the men of this particular month are attracted to dangerous endeavors, sports, speed or working for Uncle Sam. Due to their "turbocharger" personality, they are also accident-prone to the head and should protect it. They must also learn to listen to others, control impatience, focus on their needs steadily, and finish what they have started. At work, the "red" Martian personality will be felt and may hurt those who are more sensitive; thus, damaging the chances for respect and promotion.

Their explosive behavior is due mainly to an inborn inferiority complex, and they must learn not to take opposition personally. The "childlike" attitude could attract manipulative spirits wishing to structure or use the immense creativity and energy of Mars' competitive spirit. They do love home and take responsibility with their family. Nevertheless, they prefer to be where the action is. Providing they do learn patience, tolerance, and diplomacy, there is no limit where Mars will take his children. The main lessons for those born in April is to learn all the diplomatic and loving traits of the opposite, Venus-ruled sign, Libra. Those born in the month of April must assume a diplomatic attitude when dealing with others and when dealing with corporate money.

Venus Governs the Beautiful and Financially Oriented Constellation Of Taurus

Luxurious and elegant
I have the memory of an elephant
Loving all of life's finer pleasures
Gifted am I at acquiring more coffers and treasures
I am TAURUS, child of Venus.

Characteristics For Those Born In May

The month of May is governed by the affectionate planet Venus and traditionally by the reliable sign of Taurus. These souls are seen as beautiful, stubborn and practical. They are the moneymaking sign of the Zodiac. Those born in May have a lot to offer to others, providing they control their strong insecurity complex and authoritarian attitude. Taurus is gifted with organization and many are attracted to the professions of banking, real estate, the arts, computers, radio, television, psychology, aeronautics and investigation, just to name a few. Many "Bulls" will reach fortune and enjoy the security of a beautiful and big house. Strong and dominant, they have inherited a deep intuition, tremendous common sense, and a powerful will. This Venusian group must learn to control all negative thoughts about jealousy, stubbornness, and insecurity. In doing so,

Venus' constructive power can be channeled towards love, gracious mental exchanges, diplomacy; and produce the finest of all hosts and artists. However, behaving in a stubborn and unattractive manner is a serious downfall for them. Their down-to-earth approach to life must not interfere with their spiritual growth. Part of the Bull's challenge is to keep an open mind to the world of the spirit and use the metaphysical information to ensure financial growth and material security. The strong desire for riches is legendary for the souls born in May, but in some way they will also promote the New Age of Aquarius. They courageously handle the difficulties of life with a solid attitude, and the advanced ones possess nobility of purpose.

The women of this sign (like those born in November) are somewhat classic, intellectual, magnetic, sensitive and will always combine Venus' beauty and sensual magnetism to attain their goals. As a rule, Venus women are picky about their mates, so it is important that they marry someone whom is well respected. Venus, your ruler, can be surprising in her rewards to you and when she does it usually lasts forever. Keep in mind to respect the Universal Law (Moon's fluctuations), as your awareness and planning will become a major contribution to reach many of your dreams.

Mercury Governs the Nervous and Witty Dual Constellation Of Gemini

Free-thinking and intelligent
You will not find me under rigorous management
You may think you know me well
Then my other half over you casts a spell
I am GEMINI, child of Mercury.

Characteristics For Those Born In June

The witty sign of Gemini governs the month of June and traditionally is ruled by the planet Mercury. Souls reincarnated in the month of June are born intellectual, nervous, and adaptable. They are classified in Greek mythology as the "Messengers of the Gods." On the negative aspect Mercury reflects the "Lord of the Thieves" because of their double-personality characteristics. As the rule, this monthly sign does well in communications, radio, language, photography, sales, movies and any type of public relations work. Their natural zest to experience life makes them impatient and unusually nervous. They are born with a gift of youth and a quicksilver mind enabling them to adapt easily to any situation.

Once the soul learns to focus and crystallize the mind, the potential to produce interesting publications of all sorts becomes a high probability. Due to their strong desire for security, many of them are attracted to real estate and the food industry. Their financial potential is unlimited if they respect the Universal Law controlling their Second House of income. The psychological field classifies mercurial children as having "Attention Deficit Disorder" (ADD). This "disorder" is due to a strong Mercury in their chart. Incidentally, President Clinton, Einstein, and myself were born with "ADD." Contrary to what the field of psychology recognizes as an indisposition is actually a gift from God, as the soul is naturally rejecting traditional education.

Thus, if the teacher is mistaken, the Mercurial soul and his inborn sense of curiosity will help him to find the real truth, somewhere, somehow in life. Impatience, nervousness, mental curiosity, and a short attention span are the characteristics, and these have produced many a genius. Those born in June must not and will not follow long established dogmas. Whatever is taught and accepted by the majority of the students will be intellectually challenged by this natal peculiarity; thus, opening new doors to mental exploration. Promoters of common sense, you (like all air signs), have a low tolerance for stupidity. Nevertheless, basic education and discipline must be induced at an early age. Mercury (ruler of Gemini) is naturally in opposition to Jupiter (ruler of Sagittarius), which rules the codification of thoughts, dogmas, traditional education and religion. Mercury controls souls born in June and will always make them question all. Thus, expect notes from the teacher about class disturbances and your Mercury-ruled child to challenge the rules. Some of these children will, in the course of their lifetime, surprise many people

(I am one of them!). A word of caution for those born in June: Always be alert when the Moon crosses the deadly sign of Scorpio at work, especially after the Full Moon.

The Moon Governs the Nurturing and Caring Constellation Of Cancer

I am mother I nurture and provide
In my soul the physical and spiritual collide
I say, "ask and you shall receive."
But also "as you sow, so shall you reap"
I am CANCER, child of the Moon.

Characteristics For Those Born In July

The moon and the emotional sign of Cancer controls the month of July. Those born in July are strongly affected by the Moon's fluctuations, and family matters will always play an important part of their lives. They are classified as the "caretakers" of astrology. The Universal Law particularly touches this monthly sign, and their success depends on the awareness and practical use of it. Lunar children are distinctively gifted with food (cooking or eating it), real estate, and are strongly motivated by security. During the course of their lives, they usually attract to themselves a position of power or management.

Thus, financial security, if they learn to recognize and synchronize with the flux of the Moon, will allow them to shine through their ability to amass riches and possessions.

They must avoid depressive thoughts of the past and control their powerful imaginations. Steadiness, organization, warmth, love and charm belong to them. July soul's inherited powerful emotions that can be channeled positively with music, singing, and the arts in general (country music is a Cancer/July vibration.). You are attracted to successful people (older or younger mates) and many Cancerian marry rich. The natural tendency to smother family members and friends at all times makes these souls admired and deeply loved. Nevertheless, they must learn to control sensitivity and participate with life outside of the home a little more. As a rule, all Moonchildren are great homemakers unless the soul selected a non-domestic Moon position such as Aries, Leo, or Aquarius. This sign, like all water signs do regenerate in research, science, and metaphysics. Many July souls tend to worry too much about their health and should adopt a more positive spiritual attitude. A word of caution for those born in July: Learn to let go of the wrong people and move on with life. O.J. Simpson was a Cancer.

The Sun Governs the Flamboyant and Majestic Constellation Of Leo

Powerful and Charming
All things living find me disarming
I step to the center of God's stage
In the books of history I have always a page
I am LEO, child of the Sun.

Characteristics For Those Born In August

The month of August is governed by the all-powerful Sun and by the magnanimous sign of Leo. This solar sign reflects the dignified Sun's life force energy. The Sun is classified as "The Life Giver," and during the day it will outshine all the other planets. Leo souls have a lot to offer, providing they exercise control over the strong egos and authoritative nature of the untamed "King of the Jungle." Naturally gifted, those born in August are attracted to the professions involving the arts, public life, medicine, research, management, and any endeavor that could offer a form of fame in general.

Just as the Sun's rays penetrate the depths of the rainforest, you were born with the potential to bring and promote life to all that you touch. This monthly sign is fixed and strongly motivated by the will to succeed, and usually in the course of their lifetimes, Leo's do reach fame, power and fortune. Strong and dominant, those born in the constellation of Leo nurture the deep desire to organize and rule others. If the soul becomes too overbearing, he will be forced to learn and accept the lesson of humility and start right back from scratch. Destructive outbursts of emotions and unfettered pride are the enemy of the "King." He must positively direct and control the Sun's creative rays without burning himself or others.

Your challenge is to recognize the powerful Sun's energy and diligently work towards a better understanding of other creative life forces at work. Acting eccentrically and pride fully without forethought is your weakness. This monthly sign courageously handles the difficulties of life. The wise ones possess nobility of purpose. Women born in August are stunning, intellectual, magnetic, and attract others with their natural auric power. As a rule, the women of this sign are protective mothers. Still they should avoid being overbearing with their children. Health-wise, those born in August are born with a subconscious fear of death and decay, but nature gives them a strong mind and a robust body. Leo's tend to be weak and accident prone in the back, knees and joint areas (President Clinton was born in August and, busted his knee in Florida)! (A letter sent to the White House a year earlier had predicted that accident). A word of caution for those born in August: Use precaution and moderation when running or jogging.

Mercury Governs the Precise and Critical Constellation Of Virgo

Cleansing impurities large and small
Don't think yourself immune, for I see all
Attending to every chore and task
Perfection being all that I ask
I am VIRGO, child of Mercury.

Characteristics For Those Born In September

The month of September is governed by witty Mercury and by the critical sign of Virgo. Those born in September are born intellectual, picky and tend to work too hard. They can become great writers and will combine logic and intuition in dealing with life in general. They are classified as the "perfectionists" in Astrology. As a rule, Mercurial souls do well in the fields of medicine, law, teaching, writing, designing, and office work. Many of them are refined artists. The downfall of this sign is sarcasm and an overly concerned attitude with trivial matters. Some young Mercurial souls are overwhelmed with health matters, while some ignore it completely. Letting the rational mind scrutinize everything can hinder Virgo's spiritual gifts and slow down their cosmic consciousness. This sign has a natural investigative mind, and many of them are involved with science, research, radio, television, newspaper reporting, computer programming, and the law.

The advanced ones are great leaders and masters in communication. For your information, Robert Shapiro and Marcia Clark, (O.J. Simpson trial attorneys) are Virgos and indicate the potential of this sign in terms of the law. As a rule, this sign is prone to headaches or head injury, eye and sinus problems. They are strongly advised to keep away from alcohol and narcotics. On the medical side, Virgo controls the elimination principle (bowels), and they could be their worst enemy by being overly concerned with health matters. An advanced Virgo soul will soon realize that diets that are too restrictive may cause just as many problems as over-indulgence. God designed our bodies as omnivorous; thus, our metabolisms are well equipped to deal with all types of food, including red meat. If your natural desire for perfection prevails and you eliminate this "red" source of food, you must then substitute it with different red foods such as red wine, hot peppers or other thermogenic foods. The balanced diet imposed by God must be respected to avoid digestive tract problems and a loss of "power" due to a lack of energy and body heat. A word of caution: If you happen to suffer headaches or migraines, you may find relief by walking barefoot on the grass (or close to a body of water) to regenerate from the earth's magnetic field. As a rule, all souls born in September are accident prone to the head and many may die a violent death. Thus, if you were born in September, do not take chances, especially during or after the Full Moon.

Venus Governs the Diplomatic and Peaceful Constellation Of Libra

Lover of grace and harmony
Seeking the balance of matrimony
Though there are those that hold to opinions tight
I will see it in all the different lights
I am LIBRA, child of Venus.

Characteristics For Those Born In October

The month of October is ruled by the diplomatic planet of Venus and traditionally by the charming sign of Libra. Venusian souls are strongly motivated by a desire for justice and must create harmony in all areas of their lives. These individuals can easily be classified as "peacemakers" in Divine Astrology. They usually succeed in their careers due to their gentle personalities, sense of diplomacy and natural "savoir faire." They rarely learn by mistakes, but as a rule they must avoid prolonged indecision. Those born in October must respect the typical Libra's soul's purpose to achieve balance, emotional, financial, and spiritual stability during the course of their lifetime. Venus souls must learn decision making by following not only the rational mind but also their accurate intuitions. These folks possess a strong psychological aptitude, and do well in real estate, the food industry, the stock market, interior design, marriage counseling, and the arts in general. Still, they must focus on what they need first by using inner stamina and their practical and intuitive mind. These gentle personalities will be attracted to competitive people and you can expect many challenges from them.

These sensitive souls can be easily offended by the abrupt or assertive manner of business partners and should avoid taking remarks too personally. They love a good home and they like to be in the company of business-oriented partners where they can apply their tremendous diplomatic skills. Their downfall can come from their inner desire to educate themselves traditionally only. Many of them become librarians or religious leaders. As indicated by the scale, they must look at both sides of the coin and study it with both the traditional and untraditional means. In that respect, the limit of conventional education (psychology or religion) is overridden with a more advanced spiritual attitude (New Age and Astropsychology) to gain the answers they are looking for. The codification of thoughts (the law and religion) can only give them a one-sided attitude with life. To those born in October, balance and harmony can only be reached in exploring both the physical and the spiritual sides of the scale. Many of them are born philosophers and great teachers; likewise, they will travel far in search of the truth. The truth they are aiming for is right there, above their heads in the stars; not in the dogmatic books many Libras avidly read. A word of caution to those born in October: Stay clear of any and all chemicals, drugs, or alcohol. This bad habit could lead you into a hospital or worse in jail.

Pluto Governs the Mighty Constellation of Scorpio — "The Eagle or Lizard."

Holder of all the secrets deep
Never speaking for they are mine to keep
For those who plunder without care
Tread carefully for I see you there
I am SCORPIO, child of Pluto.

Characteristics For Those Born In November

The month of November is governed by the dramatic planet Pluto, and traditionally by the intense sign of Scorpio. Gifted with a powerful will, November souls are attracted to the medical profession, the police force, government and investigation, just to name a few. They are classified as the "Eagle" (positive) or the "Lizard" (negative) in Astrology. These people are very mystic and, like all other water signs, they are attracted to the study of metaphysics. Unless you are aware of their innate "negative" qualities, you are well advised to play right or keep away from them. These souls carry with them an element of life and death, and their magnetic thoughts can reach anyone, anywhere, for good or for worse. Many young Scorpio spirits will experience despair and imprisonment during the course of their dramatic lifetime. However, the destructive energies of Pluto can be channeled positively to accomplish tremendous results. This sign rules the Mafia, the police force and the absolute power of creation or destruction, including sex. The message is quite clear when representing Pluto.

No one should take chances under his command. Realizing the Eagle in them and their own birthright of creation or destruction, these souls have no known fears in the face of death. Many advanced Pluto children will "fly" well above the destructive Lizard (his destructive emotions and legendary jealousy). Those born in November can use their inborn mystical gifts to succeed were many would fail. Strong, private and dominant, they have inherited a practical mind and an acute accurate intuition.

These karmic souls must learn to control their deep emotions, and at the same time, positively direct Pluto's ultimate power for the well being of society. They do regenerate themselves with investigation, spiritual growth and must uncover their unique mission in life, as one leading others towards the undiluted truth. The women of this sign are seen in Divine Astrology as "la femme fatale." They are sensual, classic, intellectual, reserved, and magnetic; tending to use sexual power and beauty to reach their purpose. However, the powerful Scorpio is weak with affairs of the heart and tends to be in love with love. A word of caution for Scorpio: Do not use your own stinger against yourself or society.

Jupiter Governs the Philosophical and Educated Constellation of Sagittarius

I have traveled the worldwide
With naught but the law on my side
Yearning for the higher knowledge
All of God's creation as my college
I am SAGITTARIUS, child of Jupiter.

Characteristics For Those Born In December

The planet Jupiter and traditionally, the "Lucky" sign of Sagittarius govern the month of December. These souls are born philosophers, teachers, and intellectuals; they are classified as the "Truth Seekers." As a rule, Jupitarian souls do well in professions related to the codification of thought, such as teaching, computers, aeronautics, law, religion, communications, radio, and language. Many of them are attracted to holistic healing and the world of sports. Their subconscious desire to travel foreign lands will take them far away, bringing back home the results of their learning to teach the rest of us. They are born with the gift of teaching and will always promote a form of purity in life. These people tend to do quite well in office work and can be extremely organized. Folks born in December inherited from the stars a quick mind and can keep up with anyone willing to listen to them philosophize.

Once the child of Jupiter realizes the importance of education and learns to focus on chosen goals, their ruler "The Lord of Luck" will throw many blessings to them. This sign has also the potential to produce interesting books, even novels. The young Sagittarius soul is too concerned with finances and must learn to give, so that he may receive help from the accumulated good karma. They must adapt to the saying, "to be a millionaire, you must act like one." This sign rules the wilderness, the desert, and the Indians. A word of caution: Souls born with an overbearing Jupiter energy must guard against "the books;" their lesson is to realize that God cannot be confined to any man-made buildings, deities or any archaic doctrines. The advanced ones (truth seekers) will lead the rest of us towards the reality of God's manifestation through all creation. Realizing, learning, and teaching in the face of reality guides these individuals, along with the tools of the Creator; for this is a blessing, a guidance that will always direct them away from established religious dogmas; as this is their true challenge, their contribution to the world.

Saturn Governs the Power-Oriented, Structural Constellation of Capricorn

Builder of the greatest towers
Holding all the social powers
Striving to climb to the highest peak
For honor has no place for the weak
I am CAPRICORN, child of Saturn.

Characteristics For Those Born In January

Structural Saturn and, traditionally, the practical sign of Capricorn controls the month of January. Souls born in January are strongly motivated to succeed and gain a position of power in life. All are gifted with computers and possess strong organizational principles. More than any other sign, they strive for respect and position in career accomplishments. Saturn (a karmic planet) rules this sign, and these folks must avoid depressive thoughts. The part of God in ourselves is stronger than the stars we inherited, and our will must be used correctly and positively in promoting faith. Born in the middle of the winter, they will soon realize that, nothing will come easily to them. Like the symbol of the goat, slowly but surely, against all odds, the soul must climb towards the top of the mountain. Usually, the first part of life for those born in January is a constant struggle.

Only around their middle life (after many ups and downs) they usually reach a well-deserved position in their career. Saturn will reward these people late in life and will provide them with a very long life, an appreciation of all in old age, and a solid financial security. They also tend to marry as younger older partners. The fluctuation of the Moon strongly affects their moods and success in their career. A wise Capricorn will use his fish tail, be aware of the Universal Law, and synchronize his life and business with it. Steadiness, organization, patience, and charm belong to them. These people have a strong architectural or mathematical ability and their keen sense of observation will help them succeed in all of their endeavors. In the meantime, karmic Saturn will exact payment for manipulation and will throw the soul back to the painful start. January souls are attracted to successful people, and many of them marry into wealth. Emotional and sensitive, this monthly saturnine sign is quite responsible and protective of the family circle. However, they must learn to openly communicate deep feelings. Their real gifts are psychology, electronics, and careers promoted by Uncle Sam. The awareness of the natal Dragon's Head can propel those born in January to the highest position of supreme power, but their challenge is to open up to the intangible world of the spirit and its accompanying Universal rules. The natural tendency to organize people and business at all times could hinder their sensitivity with others. They are good homemakers, love real estate, and can produce great food. Trouble in 1997 came from some guilt and depression produced by important decisions involving others. Those resolutions have forced many of Saturn's children to restructure their future. As a rule these people favor a successful business environment where they can apply their tremendous organizational gifts. A word of caution for Capricorn: Be aware of those wild acquaintances willing to help you to climb the ladder of success.

Uranus Governs The Ingenious, Freedom-Oriented Constellation Of Aquarius

Holder of knowledge of the dimensions
The spark of all the inventions
Lover of all things in simplicity
Charged with the power of electricity
I am AQUARIUS, child of Uranus.

Characteristics For Those Born In February

The eccentric planet Uranus and the futuristic sign of Aquarius govern the month of February. This clan belongs to the most original souls walking this earth and has produced many inventors. This revolutionary Uranian energy rules the future, the incredible UFO phenomenon, astrology, and drives said traditionalists up a wall. Blessed by curious stars, those born in February are attracted to the professions of science, research, electronics, psychology, the police force and astrology, just to name a few. This sign rules aeronautics, advanced computers and many an Aquarian dream of becoming an astronaut. They usually reach fame and fortune during the course of their lifetime and secretly wish to master the enigmatic "time machine."

The motion picture *BACK TO THE FUTURE* is one of the best ways to represent Uranus' ingenuity in terms of creative art. Strong and fixed, they inherited from the stars an accurate intuition, tremendous common sense, and a powerful will. Yet they have to learn to listen and participate in conversations with equality. Even when the ideas being presented are not of their own making, much knowledge can be learned. Lend your full ear, do not race ahead with only thoughts of what you want to say or you will miss much. Those born in February must also learn to positively direct Uranus' innovative mental power for the improvement and well being of the world. Acting with eccentricity without forethought is a sure downfall. Aquarius' idealistic views are legendary, their soul's purpose is to promote Universal Brotherhood with the use of all technological advancement.

However, before working on others they must work on their own cosmic consciousness and awareness of the Universe. This sign handles the difficulties of life with a smile and the advanced ones transcend setback by always using the knowledge to their benefit. The women of this sign are somewhat original, independent, beautiful, and intellectual and tend to use their incredible magnetic sexuality to reach their purposes. As a rule, women born in February produce extraordinary intelligent children or twins. They are strongly advised not to eat when upset, as in the medical aspect of Divine Astrology, Aquarius is sensitive in the stomach. A word of caution for those born in February: Many young souls will not understand your spiritual message to the world and will try to hurt you.

Neptune Governs the Soft, Dreamy, Intuitive, And Artistic Constellation Of Pisces

Mystical and magical
Nebulous and changeable
I work my way up life's rivers and seas
To my place at God's own feet
I am PISCES, child of Neptune.

Characteristics For Those Born In March

Dreamy Neptune and the artistic sign of Pisces govern the month of March. These souls are born teachers, philosophers, and perfectionists and will exercise more intuition than logic in dealing with life in general. Those born in March naturally do well in holistic endeavors and many are involved in the medical profession. Those who work in construction must understand the importance of education to be able to use their celestial teaching gifts. These people are also noted for their creativity and artistic values. Michelangelo and George Washington were Pisces and used their creative attributes to the fullest. The downfall of this monthly constellation is an over preoccupation with others and a blind acceptance of religious dogmas. Nevertheless, the "good heart" of Pisces is not surpassed by any other sign of the zodiac, and the advanced ones possess spiritual healing powers. Many of the highly evolved souls born in March can lead us out of the deep clouds towards the brilliance of reality.

Their soul's purpose is to swim upstream (as represented by both fishes) towards the ethereal light of God. A young March born Pisces spirit is deceiving, complaining, and easily addicted to religious dogmas, cult endeavors, chemicals, drugs, and alcohol. This clan MUST respect the laws based on the Moon's fluctuations to avoid a negative karmic fate. This karmic March sign has within itself the potential to reach not only the light of God but also immortality, fame and fortune through artistic or spiritual work. In the medical aspect of divine Astrology, Pisces rules the feet. It is important for them to walk barefoot on the grass to regenerate the body using the magnetic fields of the earth itself. Pisces' intuition is remarkable and should be well heeded when confronted with serious decision making. A word of caution for Pisces: Your faith could take you to the deepest ugliness of those trying to control you. David Koresh and the Rev. Jim Jones are good examples.

Explanation of the Housing System

MEANINGS TO HOUSES

House 1: Outward Appearance, Soul's Purpose, Karmic Fate.
House 2: Money and Personal Possession, Self Esteem.
House 3: Brothers and Sisters, Short Trips, Private Thoughts, Studies.
House 4: Foundation, Home, Upbringing, Mother.
House 5: Love Affairs, Children, Entertainment.
House 6: Health, Service, Working Environment, Co-Workers.
House 7: Partnerships, Public, How People See You, Known, Enemies.
House 8: Legacy, Debts, Taxes, Insurance, Mortgages, Joint Resources.
House 9: Philosophies, Traveling the World, Teaching, Publishing.
House 10: Career, Superiors, Honors, Success, Father.
House 11: Friends, Hopes, Groups, Wishes, Originality.
House 12: Secrets, Occult, Subconscious, Drugs, Unknown Enemies.

The First House describes the specific soul's purpose of the individual and its private self. This includes the strength or weakness as to reach the goals and free the inherent negative qualities of the sign staging the self.

The Second House relates to energy flowing into the physical structure of the individual's private self. This includes self-esteem, sense impressions, food, possessions and money.

The Third House controls activity within the individual's private self and its mental connection to the world. The energies of this House relate to the native's sources of mental stimulation, passing on information and personal activities such as thinking, speaking, writing, errands, and hobbies.

The Fourth House describes the character of the individual's private environment. This includes the individual's home life and parents, upbringing and especially the mother. It also denotes the last resting place on this world and the attitude at home.

The Fifth House describes energy flow involving the structure of the individual's creative environment. This includes the stimulation provided by the individual's friends, social network, offspring, and entertainment. This is the House of love and attraction between human beings and its relation to children.

The Sixth House controls activity within the individual's working environment. The energies of this House describe the native's private work, type of employment, and service to others within the native's private world. This House is also directly related to the soul's health, his physical and spiritual strengths and weaknesses.

The Seventh House relates to building the self that the individual presents to the public world. It, therefore, covers legal definitions of the self such as marriage and partnerships. It controls the individual's characteristic public self-expression. This is how the soul presents itself to the world.

The Eighth House relates to the physical structure of the individual's public self. It, therefore, covers buildings and real estate. It covers energies emanating from the body so it controls sexual attraction and death. This is the House of joint resources and the business/financial potential. This House also denotes the witchcraft legacy and the potential to relearn the mysteries of life.

The Ninth House controls activity by the individual's public self. It covers mental expression and public activities such as lecturing, publishing, and traveling. This House also denotes the attitude pertaining to foreigners and foreign affair involvements.

The Tenth House relates to the character of the individual's public environment. It describes the individual's career and contribution to the world. During childhood it can describe the father.

The Eleventh House describes energy flow involving the structure of the individual's public environment. This includes altruistic, humanitarian social networking by the native. This House also depicts the type of friends the soul will attract and the attitude towards them.

The Twelfth House controls activity and change within the individual's public environment. The energies of this House describes selfless service to the public, creating work or problems for the self, activities to dissolve the self, and solitary retreat. This House regulates the potential to uncover the secret of the subconscious and how it will be used during this present reincarnation.

If a planet is positioned in a House, then the positive or negative influence generated by the celestial body will affects the flow of energy through the House. If the planet is harmoniously aspected by other planets, then the affairs of that House will flow smoothly. If the planet is under stressful aspects then the affairs of that House will be difficult. A planet in a House by its own nature affects the character of the particular life area, which the House controls. The location of the Dragon's Head or Tail in any House becomes a major contribution for success or failure in the particular Houses (See the new edition of my book, *The Power of the Dragon,* to learn more).

Astropsychology Profile
Aries

Let's start by investigating anyone that you know born in April. Those friends of yours born in April are controlled by Mars (The Lord Of War) and are very competitive, and must build and lead something of their own. This attitude gives your friends the opportunity to find their own self worth and accomplish miracles during their lifetime.

Aries, House Number 1

You know right away that with Aries you are dealing with a Fire Sign, so these souls are very competitive, not exactly patient, and they were born to lead and to control whatever they feel comfortable with. Understand also that Aries rules the head and what is inside of the head, the brain! So they all have that strong inner desire and ability to organize and to lead others. The only problem with your Aries friend is that they might not have the patience to listen to good advice, and many of them learn by making serious mistakes. But don't feel too sorry for Aries, because no matter what happens to them, they will get up and go almost immediately. It takes quite a lot to keep anyone born in April down for long. They are born fighters.

Many of them work for Uncle Sam or the government while others uses their powerful challenging spirits to build up and run their own business. Those born in April are attracted to professions that involve an element of danger, and many find themselves involved in dangerous sports such a racecar driving. They are now allowed to use their desire to lead and show the world how qualified, fast and good they really are. In the medical aspect of Astropsychology, Aries the Ram rules the head, and many of these daredevils end up with scars and broken bones. They are in some ways childlike and may need to learn the hard way of their own limits. But don't try to tell them that, your male or female friend born in April may use their powerful horns against you. Never tell them that they are no good, as the Martian spirit will work very hard to prove you wrong. Chances are that those born in April will, during the course of their life, earn a position of respect and leadership and will remember what you, once upon a time, told them. So don't make an enemy of the child of Mars, remember this planet is called in Greek mythology, the "Lord of War," and for good reason.

Aries, House Number 2

You can see that your Aries friend is no longer an Aries when it comes to the Second House of money. So now let's look at House Number 2 in the Section Housing System and read the keywords and get more information. Remember you can also refer to the Sun Sign Characteristics and read all about this Sun Sign. He or she becomes a Taurus, Taurus the Bull. The Bull, or the Sign of Taurus was chosen by the ancients to represent money and solidity. Also, many financial corporations such as Merrill-Lynch have chosen it subconsciously, because the Bull represents solidity. Incidentally this sign also rules Switzerland, where all the major banks are located. This clearly indicates that your Aries friends will know how to work with the banking system and many of them will also decide to work with cash or in a bank. And Taurus will always spend money on aesthetics and also on very expensive items. Only the best of what life has to offer for your Aries friend. So they have the potential to build up solid financial resources in working with or in the bank, your friend born in April is seriously looking for financial stability. Friends of yours born in April become Taurus in their money making schemes, but remember Taurus is a Venusian sign, and Venus rules the arts. Taurus rules music and singing, and many Martian souls will spend time and money learning and practicing the arts. While Taurus rules the earth and massage, many of those friends of yours born in April will be attracted to geology, gemology, massage, and many endeavors involving health and security. The potential to do extremely well financially is given to those born in April, but because of the speed of Mars, many will end up used or abused by her manipulative ways. Mars' speed will make them prone to trusting and ready for action almost immediately. They need to take the time in between the lines to investigate their partner to avoid costly legal disputes and losses. These people will use the genius of their Aries friend to make tons of money. However, there is such a thing as karma and nasty and abusive souls will be driven down to shame and sorrow at a much later date.

Aries, House Number 3

Now let's move to the Third House to find out how your Aries friend thinks and communicates to the world. So now let's look at House Number 3 in the Section Housing

System and read the keywords and get more information. Remember you can also refer to the Sun Sign Characteristics and read all about this Sun Sign. In this area he or she is a Gemini. Good luck to you in talking to them. It'll be difficult to make your Aries friend listen to you. They are masters in communication, but as a rule they do not necessarily listen too well to other people. Their mind is fast like lightning. They are masters with words, articulate, and gifted writers. Many of them work on radio or are leaders of a publishing company. Gemini is also the sign, traditionally ruled by Mercury, which is called the "Messenger of the Gods." Many of those born in April, (as Gemini rules) also love photography, journalism, and are adept with interpretation, translation, communication, and so forth. Some of them also work for the legal system in the courtroom where speed and accuracy is needed to report all of what is said between the lawyer, client and the judge. Some of your male or female friends born in April will also be attracted to speed and in the process get caught a few times by the police speeding. Your Aries friend's mind is like lighting and soon enough the body follows and that's why they are so fast. Many will also be classified as "Attention Deficit Disorder" (ADD) by traditional psychology. However, in the mental aspect of Astropsychology, this so-called disorder is a sure gift from the universe. Remember, Einstein, President Clinton and even myself were once upon a time classified as suffering the ADD problem. If you are interested in this phenomenon, my book ***The Power of the Dragon*** will teach you all you need to know about it. Be assured that your friends born in April are far from being limited intellectually because they don't have the patience to let you finish your sentence or listen to you for very long. That's why many of them are born fantastic writers and masters in communication. Of course the need to discipline themselves, educate themselves and read the book from the beginning will help them to achieve miracles in the world of communication.

Aries, House Number 4

Let's move on to Aries' Fourth House, which is their Home area. You know that House Number 4 rules the home area. So, who is your Aries friend at home? Well, they become a Cancer. Cancer means home, family, children, food, and real estate. So you can see that your Aries friend is very close to the family and they all want to have a beautiful home, and if possible, as Cancer is a Water sign, close to the water. And if they cannot afford a house by the ocean or a big lake or a river, well, they will have a spa or a pool or anything involving water. That could also mean, of course, a fish tank. You will also be quite surprised to realize what a good cook your male or female friend can be in the kitchen. Of course that is if they take the time to do so. My dad is an Aries and he loves to have his friends and family around and I can assure you that you would come back to his house to eat again and again. The sense of security and protection for the family is so strong that many of them are attracted and perform very well in the real estate world. The very successful ones cannot stop starting opening new restaurants and many own a lot of property. Home is important for your Aries friend, especially after a very busy day. This is where they can finally relax and enjoy their children and their secure home life. Remember you are dealing with a child of Mars, and Mars will make them active at home too. Keep in mind that they do have horns and if you upset your Aries friend, your home will become a battlefield and war will be on the daily agenda. Give them something to do and let them burn the fiery Martian energy constructively. Many of them do a lot of work around the house, and bruises, burns and cut fingers are part of their fast or dangerous endeavors. Insuring the house against fire would also be a good thing to do. Who knows, your Aries friend may decide to explore in his workshop or the garage and may blow up a few things around.

Aries, House Number 5

Time to talk about love. In their 5th House of love, romance, creativity, children and speculation, those born in April become Leo. So now let's look at House Number 5 in the Section Housing System and read the keywords and get more information. Remember you can also refer to the Sun Sign Characteristics and read all about this Sun Sign. This clearly indicates that those born in August will be attracted to those born in April. Because Sagittarius is also a Fire Sign, your Aries friends will be attracted to all the Fire Signs. Now, the universe is giving your Aries friend the opportunity to shine on stage, to lead and to create something for the world. Now, if your Aries friend decides to educate and discipline himself, the opportunity to gain fame will becomes a reality. The Sun or the Sign of Leo controls the 5th House of love, romance and speculation. During the day every planet shies away, only the bright sunshines. This clearly indicates the potential for Aries to be on the stage, to dwell very well with the arts, to do something for the light or the children. Your male or female friend born in April has been given the opportunity by the universe to provide the world with a form of light. Leo, the "King," is also quite possessive. Leo is also very, very strong and honest and will not share his queen with anybody and needs to know where she or he is at all times. So they are dramatic and that is why Aries can also be involved in acting or dancing. The sky is the limit when it comes to your Aries friends' creativity, love and romance. Don't expect your Aries friend just to sit there if he or she likes someone. Because of the Martian spirit and the desire to be first, your friend born in April will go after whom she or he likes almost immediately. Aries simply does not like to wait and are aggressive in all areas of life. To those born in April, love is also a challenge. They will be attracted to smart, beautiful, intelligent and a sexy partner. Incidentally, using their head instead of their desire to shine with a very attractive person will make them aware of a person's being on the inside. Many land on beautiful even famous partners but because Aries' desire for freedom and intellectual challenge, they do get bored sooner or later.

Aries, House Number 6

Let's now look into the Sixth House, which by the way is how your Aries friend services the world and also the way they feel about health. So now let's look at House Number 6 in the Section Housing System and read the keywords and get more information. Remember you can also refer to the Sun Sign Characteristics and read all about this Sun Sign. In this area, they do become Virgo. Virgo is the sign of "perfection." So your Aries friend becomes a perfectionist Virgo at work and with his or her body. He or she, will do paperwork, office work, organize others, and will scrutinize all details. So your Aries male or female friend will be a perfectionist at work. Unless they were born with a messy moon, they will want to see everything in perfect order and expect a clean, organized work environment. Because Virgo is the sign of health, many of your friends born in April will also tend to be overly concerned with fitness, and will worry a little bit too much about every little thing in their body. How they look and appear to their friends and world means a lot to them. Many of them will also go on a strict diet and turn themselves into vegetarians. What they are doing, is responding to the sign of Virgo, which is perfection. In that respect they will service the world with a perfectionist attitude. And they are pretty good at it. As Virgo is a hyper-critical sign, they will always find something wrong when looking at themselves in the mirror. Of course there is nothing wrong with them but this is how they do feel in private. Again, your Aries friend may be born with a moon in a water sign and retain water. Thus, they will do all they can to fix the problem and put themselves on a rigid diet to look good for themselves first. Precise, health oriented and practical, your male or female friend born in April may decide to invest in a health-oriented career and will do very well in the long run. Some suffer indigestion, even constipation, thus, they should stay away from food when they are upset with someone. Many of them are good herbalists, and many of them make beautiful clothes. Also, many like gardening around the house to vent out frustration or to service the world. With discipline they can also use their sense of perfection and become fantastic editors.

Aries, House Number 7

The 7th House reveals the way an Aries projects himself to the world and the type of business or emotional partner, like a husband or a wife that he or she will attract. See how your Aries friend would behave with business partners or his wife or in the case of a woman, with her husband. Because Aries is super-competitive and wants things yesterday, he or she will attract partners that are opposites, such as Libra's, which is the Sign in Astropsychology ruling, balance, harmony, and of course, the law. In their 7th House, your Aries friends will attract partners that are involved either with the law, or with a form of psychological gifts that help them to establish their soul's purpose. So when Aries falls on his 7th House, a Libra, he is forced to forget about himself and be more diplomatic, more sensitive to the needs of others. Adapting to the world of Libra, which is balance and harmony, will allow your Aries friends to have long-lasting relationships. As soon as they start to turn themselves into the aggressive, impatient or domineering Aries, of course they do experience stress in their 7th House of partnerships, and this attitude could invite trouble and nasty legal activities. Because Libra rules the law, your male or female friend born in April may decide to investigate the law and become an efficient attorney. To do so requires a lot of patience and discipline, but many Aries' out there do so and enjoy a very rewarding career. Others more spiritual may be inclined to explore psychology or investigate a much higher level of consciousness and become precise Astropsychologists. Your Aries friend could really surprise you with the inborn diplomacy gift they were born with, that is of course if you understand their horns and stay away from mental or physical conflicts. Adapting the opposite sign of Libra can prove to be extremely rewarding to your friend born in April. Doing so will open all the doors and with it many impressive opportunities to meet the people they need to climb the ladder of success.

Aries, House Number 8

Let's move on to the 8th House. So now let's look at House Number 8 in the Section Housing System and read the keywords and get more information. Remember you can also refer to the Sun Sign Characteristics and read all about this Sun Sign. This is the House of Corporate Money and the House of Metaphysics. Your Aries friend there becomes a powerful Scorpio, which means they do regenerate in investigations and making money. They regenerate also with corporate endeavors and investments. So, because Scorpio is a very, very deep and emotional sign, much of the trouble produced by Aries' hothead comes from their moneymaking schemes and business partners. Your male or female friend born in April does not trust people with money and will investigate them secretively. However, your Aries friend is also very spiritual and very intuitive and has a lot of potential to make a lot of money in anything and everything that involves investments, the stock market, the medical field, science and research. If you were born in April, and because of the intensity of Scorpio and the fiery temper of Aries, you are strongly advised to take all needed time before making a financial commitment with anybody. Wherever Scorpio resides in your Housing System, there is always the potential for drama even death. Thus, many Aries attract powerful money making partners and with them, the potential to build fortunes. Aries also knows the importance of insurance and many works in that area. Scorpio rules sex, and Aries is a turbo charged sign. The sexual drive and appetite is very strong. On a negative side, many young Aries souls, as this House rules corporate money and sex, ends up using sex for financial reward. And many prostitutes born in April met their spiritual and physical death in the kingdom of the night with the worse element of our society. On a more productive side, the advanced Aries will use the Scorpio 8th House of life and death productively and will become precise doctors and nurses. Some other Arian and wise souls born in April may also explore the metaphysical world and serve society accordingly. Your male or female friend born in April has been given the potential to bring about wealth and share it with others. Aries was born to lead and many are powerful financial leaders in the financial world.

Aries, House Number 9

Let's move on to the 9th House of your Aries male or female friend. In some ways it indicates, how and what they will experience, in terms of higher education, dealing with foreigners and publishing. Now, let's see how your Aries friend feels about education, traveling and foreigners. In this area of their life, your friend born in April becomes a Sagittarius, which means they will attract people from foreign lands and will do well in publishing. They will educate themselves traditionally, as Sagittarius rules colleges and universities. They will also travel far physically and spiritually, and no matter how impatient they are, they will always take the time to sit and read many books. The opportunity to reach and teach the world through publishing is given to them. So, many Aries also have the potential to do very well in foreign lands, in translating their work, or in dealing with publishing. They love traveling, some will be forced by fate to explore the Indian world and participate in structuring their legal rights. Other Aries souls will dwell with animals and may decide to become veterinarians. Aries is an explorer and taking a chance in the Amazon, Africa or any of the world's rainforests will not scare them. They do strive for adventure and action. Keep in mind that you could be any other sign of the zodiac and still feel this way. That is because in your astrological chart, you carry a very strong Aries energy. Unless you dwell with a proficient

Astropsychologist, you may not exactly understand why, you're not born in April, but because and not knowing it, your moon or your Dragon's Tail is in Aries, you have a lot to do with this sign. So your male or female friend born in April is an adventurer at heart and if he or she cannot travel physically, rest assured that the books they read will take care of the situation. As Aries is classified as "the baby" of the zodiac and the Ninth House in Sagittarius rules the codification of thoughts, many young souls will fall for a specific religion and will try to impose their religious way of life on to others. The wiser souls are well aware of the manipulation involving organized religion and will fight to death to promote the celestial truth involving the stars.

Aries, House Number 10

The 10th House of your Aries male or female friend is in the Sign of Capricorn. So now let's look at House Number 10 in the Section Housing System and read the keywords and get more information. Remember you can also refer to the Sun Sign Characteristics and read all about this Sun Sign. Your Aries friend becomes a Capricorn in their career endeavors. Capricorn is a goat that has a very high mountain to climb against the wind and the cold and the snow, which indicates that nothing will be given to your Aries male or female friend. He has to go all the way up against all odds and work really hard. But Saturn, the ruler of Capricorn, will give in sooner or later, and reward them with distinction and a position of control. Keep in mind that the stars do not think, they simply do and cannot rationalize with the spirit. Thus, your friend born in April may decide to become a leader in any chosen field, for good of for worse as far as humanity is concerned. Saturn, when the time is right, will put them in a position of management and control. So, regardless of his endeavors, progressive or not, your Aries friend has the potential to establish a very strong career and get honors and respect in society. Now Capricorn also means working for or against the government. Capricorn is the head of the goat, it's the sign chosen by Christianity to represent the head of the devil. This sign has a strong potential for structure, engineering and architecture, and many souls born in April do extremely well in structures and with the government. On the negative side the sign of Capricorn rules manipulations and abuse, and on the positive side, respect, decency and responsibility. Many of your male and female friends will be attracted to traveling and will choose to perform in the Navy or the Army. This type of career would give them the potential to lead others into the battlefield after a long and well-deserved service to the country. Many successful governmental figures were born in April and spent much of their lives fighting or organizing others to protect their country of birth. Slowly but surely, your male or female friend born in April will make an impact to the world by standing high and respected on the top of a mountain, as represented by Capricorn, the goat.

Aries, House Number 11

In the wishes and friends area, your Aries male or female friend will attract those born in February and those born in August. These unique souls will further in their own way, Aries' wishes. As always, look at the Section Housing System for House Number 11 and read the keywords. See now what type of friend he will attract and how your Aries friend will treat his friends. Aquarius is the Sign that rules everything to do with electronics, computers, television, radio, astrology, UFOs, the impossible, and the incredible. This sign loves to travel the world and may decide to put your Aries friend on television or the radio world. Aquarius rules the future and new endeavors, and many of your Aries friends have the wish to invent something. So souls born in April have wishes to travel the world and to explore the impossible and the incredible. And those born in February and August will give Aries the potential to have their wishes come true. Traveling the world physically or spiritually is something they want to do, and many an Aries will be attracted to perform where action, danger and traveling are a part of the task. Your male or female friend born in April cannot do without friends, they need to talk and communicate with them on a regular base. They will attract weird friends and may lose their personalities by adapting to those weird friends, just to be like them. However, those born in April are very different by nature and melting in a negative group and their endeavors will diminish their potential to lead. Your male or female friend born in April was not born to be a follower but was born to lead others. Providing the group of friends they belongs to is progressive, not a destructive gang for example, they could do miracles for the world. Sadly enough, however, Aries, ruled by Mars (the red planet), is the planet that also rules war, danger and fire. Many young Aries souls have fallen and lost their precious lives in the name of the group. Promoting the Aquarius Universal love, freedom and respect of others will always give your Aries friend the potential to lead others into productivity, peace, love and harmony.

Aries, House Number 12

Let's now look at the 12th House and that is the subconscious area or the fears of your Aries friend. Look at the Section Housing System for House Number 12 to understand the keywords. Your Aries male or female friend's secret fears are in this House, and you can then realize how he or she feels about life in general. Here, he or she becomes a soft Pisces. Indeed, Pisces is a very karmic sign and will either swim upstream towards freedom, knowledge, faith, and happiness, or downstream towards fear, chaos, the past, guilt or deception. So your Aries friend may have a subconscious fear of not being good enough. Your Aries male or female friend may have the subconscious fear of ending up alone — not loved or crazy. Irrational fears coming from the subconscious do not necessarily mean that they will take place. Pisces is a Water Sign, and because it has no solid grounding, the imagination will play an important part in the subject's inner life. It simply indicates that much of the fears of your male or female Aries friend are most of the time unfounded. If your Aries friend decides subconsciously to swim upstream there is absolutely no limit to where he or she will end up on the ladder of success. Intuitive, caring, loving, sensitive, artistically oriented, those born in April have a depth of feelings for life and for others. In times of trouble, wake them up and tell them that they are great, competitive, and have a lot to offer to the world. Make sure they do not fall for the negative fish and try to take them out of the quicksand they are prone to fall in. Remember, Pisces rules religion, and many young Aries souls have been poisoned at a young age and will build up fear of an imaginary devil. Some may assume that they will end up in hell forever and won't be allowed to see and rejoin those gone before or after them. Because Pisces and Neptune rule religion and deception, more than any other sign, your Aries friend is very prone to fall for any religion. However, in times of trouble, if you help your Aries friend to free his subconscious from evil thoughts, chances are that he or she will work hard to promote your own happiness and success.

At this point there is not much that your male or female Aries friend can hide away from you, so let's go now into the sign of Taurus and explore anyone you know born in May.

Astropsychology Profile Taurus

Let's now investigate souls born in May. Venus (The Goddess of Love) rules the sign of Taurus. Those born in May are solid, beautiful and competitive and must establish emotional, financial and spiritual stability in their life. They can be quite stubborn, and this attitude gives your Taurus friend the opportunity to never stop building and achieving fame and fortune.

Taurus, House Number 1

The Bull was chosen by the ancients to represent money, stability and security. Switzerland is a Taurus country, and one of the reasons why all the wealthiest and powerful banks are located there. The soul's purpose of a Taurus, as represented by the Bull, is to establish emotional, financial and spiritual stability. The keywords for Taurus are "I have" and "I possess." So of course they can be quite reluctant to let go of things or people when their mind is made up. And they too have horns like Aries so be careful not to upset a Bull, because you may be in trouble if you do so. Simply look at the buffalo in Africa, indeed the bull is one of the most tenacious and ferocious and is not even afraid of lions. One of their lessons in life is to learn to let go of the wrong people or the wrong things when bad times come. Your male or female friend born in May simply sees you as one of their possessions. Taurus' are built to last. Because Venus, which is the planet of love and rules this sign, they are beautiful, they will love candlelight, romance, and good food. Those born in May are artistically inclined. If the Bull uses his big heart instead of his mind, he or she may land on a person below their expectations or their station in life. Then Taurus will be very unhappy not to enjoy the finer things in life and will get very depressed. However, if your male or female friend born in May is also very intuitive and if he or she sees the potential for success, the Bull will take over and provide all the needed help for his or her partner to succeed. He or she will work harder than any other sign to bring about all the good things that life has to offer. The Bull might be slow to act, but he is very steady and will not be afraid of any challenge in front of him. His powerful horns and massive body gives the Bull the potential to move mountains and you, if you happen to be in his way! Like its counterpart the Buffalo, in the wild or at home, Taurus loves to be in the pack and will fight to the death to protect his family. Regardless of its legendary possessiveness, once a decision about a person or a challenge has been made, the Bull can easily turn away and look somewhere else for happiness.

Taurus, House Number 2

Now look and read the keywords for House Number 2. In his Second House of possession, your Taurus friend becomes a Gemini. Gemini rules everything to do with communications, writing, radio, and television which indicates in many ways the potential given to those born in May to do extremely well in the world of communications. And of course, as the Bull is the sign of wealth, they have inherited a dual personality when it comes to make money, and they have numerous ways and different means of making it. Many of them work in radio, sales, real estate, and travel agencies. They run a lot of errands and drive around the city making tons of money. Because Mercury rules transportation and cars, some of your Taurus friends will operate in those areas. Most of all they are gifted speakers and great writers. Mercury, the planet ruling Gemini becomes a Taurus in this section of their life. In order to fulfill their soul's purpose and amass riches, your male or female friend born in May will read and educate himself with books about money and solid investments. Remember, Venus the planet of love and beauty also rules Taurus. Thus, your male or female friend born in May loves shopping. They are looking for the best that money can buy and are adept in finding the best deals around. Taurus hates wasting money and if they do invest in a product or involve themselves in a financial endeavor, you can be sure that they did not overlook anything. I know a lot of students and clients born in May and these souls operate in some way in the field communications. One of my close friends works as a radio host at a local radio station. In the case of the famous television host, Jerry Springer, he was born in May and he is surely adept in communication. Taurus is a refined sign and loves perfumes. Many work in retail stores selling high-class products, or in a bank where they handle cash on a daily basis. Because Gemini is a communications sign, your male or female friend born in the month of May will talk quite a lot about money and what to do to make more. Often they provide a helping hand to their brothers and sisters to deal with the difficulties of life. Because Mercury rules transportation the wealthy souls born in May will be attracted subconsciously to invest in very expensive artwork or cars.

Taurus, House Number 3

Let's look at how your Taurus friend thinks. So now let's look at House Number 3 in the section Housing System and read the keywords and get more information. Remember you can also refer to the Sun Sign Characteristics and read all about this Sun Sign. Cancer is the sign that rules everything to do with home, family, food, real estate, mommy, daddy, apple pie, and baseball. So you're talking about someone naturally concerned with security and many of them have food on their mind all the time. Some, expecting the apocalyptic time, will make sure to store away enough dry food to survive for months. Of course this apocalyptic junk will never happen but many people born in May will do what their stars want them to do and put away food for the so-called hard days. Intuitive, sensitive, and caring, your Taurus male or female friend is family oriented. Venus, the planet of love could over indulge them with the greatest things life can offer, thus, they do need to exercise to feel good and to lose some weight. Their mind is also concerned with home where they can cook and entertain their close friends. If you have a friend born in May, take good care of him, as he will in turn take care of you. He or she will do that with great love, attention, and most of all luxury. Because the 3rd House rules the mind and Cancer rules general security, many souls born in May will invest in real estate. Many are quite successful, and many run auspicious hotel and restaurant businesses. Understand that the Moon rules this House, thus, your male or female friend born in May can suffer the Moon's fluctuations and become a bit "lunatic" or depressed in times of a waning moon. Do not try to fool them, as Cancer is a very receptive sign. Their intuition is quite developed and they can read through you. Even though Taurus is an earth and practical sign, the mind in Cancer is set to dwell very well with spiritual matters. Many of these souls born in May are also involved and do quite well in New Age endeavors. The mind of a Taurus is set to offer protection, food, security and total commitment to those they care for. Do not forget that Cancer is also a shrewd business sign, thus, your male or female friend born in May will naturally know where and how to make good money.

Taurus, House Number 4

Let's move on to their home area or their base of operation, or the 4th House. Use the Housing System for keywords and read how your Taurus friend will behave at home. In this area Taurus becomes a Leo. As you know,

Leo is ruled and controlled by the Sun, which means an opportunity given to those born in May to own and shine in their beautiful home. That is why they need a beautiful home with expensive artwork. Remember Leo rules France, so they will have either French artwork or Italian artwork, as Leo rules these countries. And that is why we say French and Italians are romantic. And it even affects our language making it very romantic. Being a Leo at home indicates a potential for your friend, born in May to throw parties and to be a channel for love. In their home they can find light in creating things of their own. Many of them also shine in real estate endeavors and enjoy showing and selling expensive properties. Big houses where a lot of beautiful and expensive things are displayed will indicate Taurus' base of operations, and because they are Leo, they will want to show the world their beautiful possessions. Also, because Leo rules children, your male or female friend born in the month of May will be a magnet for children. Leo is also born to be a boss, thus, they will not tolerate undisciplined children. Meantime, Taurus was born with the gift to direct and promote the best in any child. Some of them run institutions where lost or deprived children can get a chance to adjust to life. Their particular gift is also to teach the arts to those children, especially music and singing. Those born in May must establish security and love and will do just that for themselves and those they care for. The advanced ones use hi-tech means to write and produce fantastic books for children. The creative potential is very strong and starts in their private home. The universe is offering your male or female friend born in May to shine right from there, at home. Ultimately, your friend born in May will manage to get a beautiful home and will regenerate in furthering the light of the Sun. The children of the world will be the first ones to benefit from Taurus' creativity.

Taurus, House Number 5

Let's move on to the 5th House of love and romance, to see what your Taurus male or female friend becomes when he or she is touched by love. Refer to the Section Housing System and learn more of the keywords. Well, they are Virgo with love and Virgo is the sign of perfection. So, Taurus' attract Virgos and another Earth Sign, Capricorn. They are perfectionists. They are constantly looking at you. Make sure that you look nice and you smell nice, and that you are healthy. Virgo is the sign that regulates health. And they want their lovers to be hard workers and responsible, as Virgo rules productivity. So in many ways they are very critical of the people they choose to be with because what they are aiming for is purity and solidity. They are looking for somebody that will stay with them forever. Remember the Bull means solidity and security. And it is the same with their heart. Now by being too fussy and too picky, they could hurt their love relationships, as nobody is perfect. Taurus needs a lot of plants around them and as Virgo rules healing, many of them will work naturally with plants. Like Taurus, Virgo is an earth sign and many do well in archeology, geology, and gemology. In some ways, because Taurus rules money and possessions, many will strive to own expensive rare rocks such as emeralds or diamonds. Your Taurus male or female friend may also surrender to the critical sign of Virgo and many of those born in May could be overly concerned with their appearance or their health. Taurus was born with a strong constitution and like the Bull has big bones. But because Taurus is slow in nature, they must keep active to burn the water they retain in their flesh and cells. Many will harass themselves by letting the overly critical sign of Virgo see things that others will not even notice. Tell them how beautiful and great they really are and your Taurus friend will love you forever. However, remember they are very sensitive and intensely intuitive, but they can handle the truth. Thus, be diplomatic about saying what is on your mind about their appearance and back it up with positive suggestions. Many will turn themselves into vegetarians just to feel good about themselves. But don't expect it to last, as the lust for the good things in life will take over sooner or later.

Taurus, House Number 6

Let's move on to the 6th House of work and service to the world. In this area your Taurus male or female friend becomes a Libra. So now let's look at House Number 6 in the Section Housing System and read the keywords and get more information. Remember you can also refer to the Sun Sign Characteristics and read all about this Sun Sign. Libra means the law of both the physical and spiritual worlds. Libra also means psychology or Astropsychology in a much higher level of perceiving the human mind interaction with the Universal Mind. This is what you are learning right now. At work, your Taurus friend will need partners and their long lasting endeavors will be sealed by contracts. So Taurus is set to be naturally diplomatic in working and performing with other people. Your male or female friend born in May is also willing to enter into any contracts and to work or to service a group as long as it makes solid sense to them. Taurus is attracted to the arts mostly because Venus, the planet of love and beauty rules the sign of Taurus, and Venus, the planet of music and acting rules Libra. Thus, in many ways, your Taurus friend needs a beautiful environment to work, create, perform or sing. The 6th House rules also health, which means their environment at work must be well balanced and beautiful. If the people they are dwelling with are rude or use rough language or behave in an unprofessional manner, your male or female friend born in the month of May will be very unhappy. Taurus' health depends on a well-adjusted and positive atmosphere. Anything else will make the bull use his dangerous horns and move away to a better environment. Intuitive, sensitive, creative, and diplomatic by nature, your Taurus friend is well fitted to dwell within a group where they can provide tremendous guidance to those in need. Some, more earthy by birth, may decide to educate themselves traditionally and work in the legal field where their ability to deal with people will open many worthwhile doors to success. As a rule, your male or female friend born in May will not sign or commit himself to a job or a position without serious consideration. However, when this is done, your Taurus employee will be one of the most efficient power forces you could ever dream of. The sign of money and security will ultimately bring you, the boss or the lucky friend, great rewards in the long run.

Taurus, House Number 7

Let's move on to the 7th House of marriage and the way those born in May present themselves and whom they will attract in their world. Take the time to explore House Number 7. Your Taurus friend becomes a Scorpio, a very sensual and powerful water sign. The sign of Scorpio rules sex, magnetism and passion. That's why those born in November will find those born in May quite irresistible. Scorpio has a lot of passion and its stinger can be devastating to the partners who would dare to upset a Bull. On a more positive note, your friend born in May has the potential to attract devoted and emotional partners. Money, wealth and power will be the regular topic, as both Taurus and Scorpio are gifted with finances. So Taurus becomes a Scorpio with others. This water sign knows where money is, because Scorpio is known as the investigator. Those born in May face the world as a Scorpio and they become very intuitive and powerful investigators of the zodiac. But again, becoming a Scorpio with others, your Taurus friend becomes really intense. This is a dramatic sign, and Scorpio has a deadly stinger. So when Taurus becomes jealous, too possessive, suspicious and argumentative, he stings to death his marriage or his business relationships. So your Taurus friend has to learn, of course, to trust people a little bit more. But again, it is because they want their business or love to last forever. They have to realize that life is a process of constant changes. Nothing really lasts forever. Meantime there is the potential to find long lasting partners, that is, if the partner they are with inherited a compatible star pattern. Because Taurus turns himself into a Scorpio in public, your male or female friend becomes a sensual magnet to the world. Their sensual aura is so magnetic that they can induce sexual thoughts to others just by walking around. On a negative note, Scorpio rules drama and death and many Taurus souls will have to endure a form of life and death experiences in some of their unhealthy relationships. Powerful, committed, magnetic, and intuitive, if you sign a contract with a Taurus, stand all the way with them, and you will never be sorry you did so.

Taurus, House Number 8

Let us move on to the 8th House of corporate money, or the business bank account, or the partner/husband potentials to make money. So now let's look at House Number 8 in the Section Housing System and read the keywords and get more information. Remember you can also refer to the Sun Sign Characteristics and read all about this Sun Sign. This 8th House is into the world of Sagittarius. This means that Taurus can do very well in publishing, and can produce fantastic teachers and writers. Some of their work can also be translated and enjoyed by foreign people. This is because Sagittarius on the 8th House regulates foreigners. Taurus rules Switzerland where all the banks are located. So your Taurus friend is prone to open a bank account, maybe a secret bank account in a foreign land and do extremely well financially outside of his or her home country. Scorpio rules metaphysics, while Sagittarius rules the codification of thoughts and religion. It is important for them to realize that, the truth they are desperately looking for, is not necessarily printed in the books they have read. Thus, Taurus must learn to let go of established doctrines and aim for a more advanced, even spiritual material. They must realize that the truth they are longing for is in the stars, as much of the rational material they deal with may not satisfy their curiosity. This House also governs the Indian world and animals. Many souls born in May also enjoy spending money traveling, and gambling is part of their less glamorous endeavors. Still, they are lucky on the gaming table and many do hit the jackpot. Traditionally the 8th House is ruled by Scorpio, thus, your male or female friend born in May will travel far physically and spiritually to satisfy their powerful thirst for sex, money making schemes or spiritual investigations. Many wealthy Bulls also invest in foreign cultures, and not knowing better, support Neptunian or religious organizations. Taurus is an earth sign and long to sustain long establish doctrines. Advanced souls do make good use of their financial resources and invest in New Age endeavors to further freedom and the truth essence of the spirit.

Taurus, House Number 9

The 9th House is how your Taurus male or female friends will explore education. Dig into House Number 9 for some keywords. In the educational field, your friend born in May becomes a practical, serious and dedicated Capricorn. This House of education is ruled and controlled by Saturn and Saturn will force your Taurus friend to climb high mountains slowly to get to the top of higher education. So Taurus is willing to work hard. Sometimes they educate themselves a little bit late because Saturn freezes the area, but sooner or later, through their powerful stamina and indestructible will, the stubborn Bull, will get to the top and get recognition. Taurus' desire for stability and financial security is very strong. Thus, it makes sense to them to invest time and money in school. In that respect, after a long education, the reward and title will make them earn more money. Meantime, your friend born in the month of May must recognize also that there is a big difference between education and intelligence. Whatever he or she has been taught does not necessarily mean it is the truth even if the majority accepts it. In many ways your male or female Taurus friend is sensitive enough to detect the truth wherever the truth is. This education House, ruled by Capricorn will bring your Taurus friend to work for large, well-established organizations or his local government such as the city or even Uncle Sam. In order to establish a long-lasting job, a Taurus will educate himself and may decided to work for the government or run their business. Working for Uncle Sam will give your male or female friend born in May, the sense of security to retain a long lasting position. Sometimes Taurus also realizes that Uncle Sam's paycheck may be steady but it is also meager. Many change career in the latter part of their life and re-educate themselves with electronics, computers and the media (such as in Jerry Springer's case, turning himself from the mayor of a city into a very successful television host.) Now the money flows and Taurus can enjoy the best of the best, even if it is a bit late.

Taurus, House Number 10

Let's move on to the 10th House of career. Look at the Housing System and read the career area Number 10. The Sign of Aquarius rules the 10th House of career of your Taurus friend. Again, I am sure many of you have heard of Jerry Springer. Well, Jerry is a Taurus, and Aquarius rules anything and everything to do with electronics and television. So, in the 10th House of career, those born in May, will have to use or be brought to deal with electronics and computers, the media etc. Jerry did and will fly far and fast to establish his second career. Keep in mind that Aquarius rules eccentricity and weird things. I believe there is plenty of that on Jerry Springer's national televised show. Taurus somehow will have to service the world sometimes in an original way. That is why you have a lot of people born in May, male and female that are into the New Age and many of them work as airhostesses and pilots. Incidentally, Aquarius rules the future, electronics, and a plane is nothing else than a large piece of electronic equipment with wings. Your male or female friend born in May could also dream of becoming an astronaut or an inventor. Because Venus, the planet of the arts rules Taurus, many people born in May will also display their talents on television. Other creative Bulls may also profile their genius in electronics and work in the world of computerized Aquarius and television. Many of the best broadcasters were born in May and many dwell with the future. Lots of advanced Taurus' operate, and speak at New

I Know All About You 57

Age conferences, and many, no matter how earthy they are, delve into the UFO phenomenon. In this career area, your male or female Taurus friend becomes an Aquarius, and Aquarius deals with the extraordinary. This sign rules astrology, thus, many of my successful students were born in May and enjoy a great career as Astropsychologists. Aquarius rules flying and traveling the world, and many of you born in May will have to travel far and fast. Aquarius also rules Japan and many Taurus souls will visit those islands. Your male or female friend born in May are rational and practical, but the Universal Mind will gear many of them to work and promote the future thought through the world of Aquarius, in their 10th House of career endeavors.

Taurus, House Number 11

So now let's look in the wishes and friends area for those born in May. So now let's look at House Number 11 in the Section Housing System and read the keywords and get more information. Remember you can also refer to the Sun Sign Characteristics and read all about this Sun Sign. Your Taurus friend will attracted Pisces and Virgo friends, but at the same time Pisces, as you learned earlier, is also a little bit deceiving, which means Taurus uses too much of his or her heart with friends. They should use a bit more of their heads and make demands on some of those friends to check them out. Many negative fish swimming down-stream will take the bull for a ride. So, if you were born in May, do not feel guilty if you cannot help a friend. Some of those so-called friends could be Neptunian and deceive you into the wrong road, the wrong behavior, the wrong friends and the wrong actions. But at the same time, the positive fish indicates friends that are very spiritual and artistically oriented. Some will be musicians, dancers, powerful metaphysicians, astrologers, and psychics. So becoming a Pisces, a water sign in the House of wishes, many Taurus' will cruise the world of Neptune or Poseidon, the Lord of the Sea, to an exotic island and enjoy the best that life can offer. And as a good friend, you will also enjoy the ride on the waves. Taurus is the sign of wealth and an exotic place will always appeal to them, especially if they can enjoy good food and a great massage. If you were born in May, make sure not to let Neptune dry out your wishes by simply dreaming about all the good things that life has to offer. If there is a sign that can do it, that's you. But you must be practical about it and realize that you are on a physical world. This world demands you to work at it and socialize more to reach the friends that can promote your wishes. Many of your friends born in May dream of becoming billionaires and cruise to many exotic islands (that is until they do find the perfect one to relax with after a life of hard work). Chances are they will do it if they simply ask in order to receive emotional, financial and spiritual stability. If you have a friend born in May, once more treat him or her real well. As a good friend, you will be asked to be a part of their long lasting dream.

Taurus, House Number 12

So now let's look in the subconscious are and see what's in the back of the head of your friend born in May. So now let's look at House Number 12 in the Section Housing System and read the keywords and get more information. Remember you can also refer to the Sun Sign Characteristics and read all about this Sun Sign. Your Taurus friend becomes an Aries. And that is why you don't want to upset the Bull because this sign has horns too! Two sets of horns can do serious damage, but used wisely they will make your friend born in May extremely competitive. They are constantly looking for new ideas to make money and they want to be first in doing so. Being first means also the potential for monopoly and lead the market before anyone. Your friend born in May will also learn by mistake and realize the importance to share information and action with those they do trust. Many have lost great business opportunities to make millions because of the greed or insecurity produced by the Aries spirit. The more advanced souls born in the month of May will strive to find their true relationship with the universe. Then, when he or she finally finds their godly powers, the sky becomes the limit. Subconsciously, your Taurus friend wants to prove to the world and to himself that they have what it takes to establish genuine security so that they can live a great life. Secretively, Taurus is also longing to find the deep meaning of life. Once the objectives and wealth are reached, your male and female friend born in May, will wonder if he can take some of it for his next reincarnation. The sense of security and possession is so strong that losing a friend or a business can destroy a Taurus. All the valuable spiritual information will help the Bull to learn to let go of the wrong people and to value and accept the unavoidable changes. Your Taurus friend may appear slow in this physical world, but don't be fooled, for he is as fast as lighting in his subconscious motivation. This spiritual awareness will help Taurus to stand against the strongest wind and face life's challenges with faith. There is not much your male or female Taurus friend cannot do especially when he or she sets their mind to do so. They might be slow in some areas of life, but with a pair of horns in front of them, who wants to stop them?

Astropsychology Profile
Gemini

Mercury (The Messenger of the Gods) rules souls born in June. Their conventional Sun Sign is the "Twins" or Gemini. This gives your Gemini friends the opportunity to explore a dual life. Gemini is also the sign of communications, curiosity and critical /thinking.

Gemini, House Number 1

The soul's purpose of your friends born in June is to explore the duality of life. Gemini is ruled and controlled by Mercury, called in Greek mythology the "Messenger of the Gods." Gemini rules also radio. A radio host called Mr. Art Bell is a good example to represent the planet Mercury. Mr. Art Bell is a Gemini born in June. And what does he do? He talks all the time for a living. Gemini is the sign of communications and your male or female friend born in June was born to communicate. You may also find a quiet Gemini that is because he or she inherited at birth, an introverted moon or a Dragon position in a feminine, shy and calm sign. As a rule, Gemini's have a double personality and it is represented by the symbol of the twins in the zodiac. The female in the sign represents Gemini's creativity, sensitivity and artistic values. The male represents a more aggressive and undisciplined side of the sign. Because the universe wants your male or female friend born in June to experience a double life, many will look much younger than they really are. This rule applies to any sign of the zodiac, hence, if you know someone not born in June but who looks younger than his or her age, you can be sure that this person was born with a Moon or a Dragon's Head or Tail in Gemini. Thus, the numbers two, four, six, and eight will follow them throughout their lifetime. Many will have two children, have been married twice, have two homes, are from a different country, speak two languages, etc. Your male or female friend may also get confused and will try hard to finish what he or she starts. They do get bored really fast and need to discipline themselves and finish their education. Many of them end up as "jack of all trades" but don't feel bad for them, they usually change career at least four times in their life. Change is the essence of life for a Gemini. They do get really bored with routine and need plenty of challenges. They are particularly good with their hands and many are gifted mechanics. The female side of a Gemini may also take over and lead your Gemini friend into the arts, photography, the medical field or public speaking. If they discipline themselves early enough, a Gemini can become a fantastic writer or a prominent speaker.

Gemini, House Number 2

Let's look in the money area for those born in June. So now let's look at House Number 2 in the Section Housing System and read the keywords and get more information. Remember you can also refer to the Sun Sign Characteristics and read all about this Sun Sign. Gemini's 2nd House is in the Sign of Cancer, which means that those friends of yours, or family members, born in June will always put some money away for the hard days. Cancer rules housing, clothing, food, hotels, restaurants, and real estate. Many people born in June are natural salesmen, some also work in real estate, in hotels, and restaurants. Others work as bartenders, waiters and waitresses. The ability to disguise themselves and talk about so many different topics helps them to make new friends fast. At a restaurant clients will do all they can to sit in the section of your Gemini friend, and tend to tip them well. A busy public place is a perfect choice for a Gemini, especially night work where smoke, noise and action reign. The speed and swift thinking they were born with is the perfect gift needed to talk and service the people around them. A really good friend of mine, Johnny was born in June. He graduated from a well known culinary school of French cuisine in Paris, and he became a fantastic pastry chef. He has been working for Hyatt Hotels for many years now. Let me give you another example of a real good friend of mine born in June, his name is Owen. He spent all his life as a contractor and built many homes. Remember Cancer rules home, family, and general security. Other souls born in June work for Uncle Sam in the Army and the Navy and service their country. America, July 4th, 1776 is a Cancer country. The desire to travel far and fast is always present and that is why your male or female friend born in June gets bored with routine. Working for the government will give them a sense of fulfillment and will allow them to travel around the world. Even if you think that your Gemini friend is indecisive, he or she is very responsible with money and will always stash some away for the hard days. Your male or female Gemini friend is always concerned with security and will go to a great length in helping his or her family members. Understanding and respecting the Universal Law, based upon the Moon's fluctuations will become a major contribution to establish financial security and invest wisely. More on this law is to be found in my book, *The Power of the Dragon.*

Gemini, House Number 3

In their 3rd House, ruling the thinking process, your friends born in June become a Leo. So now let's look in this area for those born in June. So now let's look at House Number 3 in the Section Housing System and read the keywords and get more information. Remember you can also refer to the Sun Sign Characteristics and read all about this Sun Sign. This means an opportunity given to the Gemini soul to shine through his words. That is why you have a lot of very famous radio hosts that shine in the world of communications and get famous through the world of Leo. Again, famous radio host Art Bell is a Leo in his mind. However, on a negative aspect, the creative force of the Sun can also burn and will turn your male or female Gemini friend into a bossy Leo. Spiritual pride could also harm their speech and many listeners may find the radio host verbally aggressive or impatient with the guest. But as a rule, your Gemini friend does mean well. The Sun or Leo rules love, romance, children, friends and the light. Also the Sun rules anything and everything that has to do with the stage and creativity. Some of the best speakers in politics or in the broadcasting industry have a strong and well-developed Leo in their Third House of communication. President Clinton, and former Speaker of the House, Newt Gingrich, were both born with a Dragon's Head in Gemini. Thus, President Clinton addresses the country each day using the radio to bring us the "National Address." Many famous writers, such as Salman Rushdie were also born with a Dragon's Head in Gemini. The potential to do well in the world of communication, learning, teaching, and publishing is given to them. Many souls born in June are also great translators or court reporters. The duality involving this sign will force the soul to dwell with foreigners and many will end up moving, marrying and living in foreign lands. Your male or female friend born in June is an artist, thus, Leo will make them prone to learning and mastering the arts. Some of them will tap into their birth gift and will promote light, love, and life to others. Because Leo rules children, your Gemini's friend mind will always be concerned with giving and protecting children. Many of them travel the world and are doing a fantastic work doing so. The mind of a Gemini is a solar mind loaded with jokes and honest laughs. Your male or female friend born in June will never really grow up, and it is this sense of life and light that makes them so popular with everybody.

Gemini, House Number 4

So now let's look in House Number 4 for those born in June. In the home area, your male or female Gemini friend becomes a Virgo. So now let's look at House Number 4 in the Section Housing System and read the keywords and get more information. Remember you can also refer to the Sun Sign Characteristics and read all about this Sun Sign. This is the sign of perfection. Virgo means organization, paperwork and classification. So your friend born in June needs to have a very organized environment where the opportunity to structure and organize will induce creativity. Virgo rules plants, herbs and greenery in the wild, and of course, the rainforest. Those born in June need to surround themselves with the color green and plants. Meantime, if a less organized Moon or Dragon afflicts the chart, your Gemini friend is much to busy to organize his home life and can operate in a total mess. He is the only one who can find his own stuff in a pile of paperwork or toys. Like Gemini, Virgo is a sign ruled by Mercury. Thus, the opportunity to edit, write and communicate from home is given to the soul. Learning and using computers can be a very good thing for your Gemini friend. The disciplines found in the hi-tech industry (hard-drives/computers) can seriously enhance your Gemini friends' creativity right from home. Virgo also rules clothing, and many Gemini's love to own a lot clothes and to go shopping. Some of their outfits will be used to go camping and the more delicate ones will be worn when socializing. Many Gemini writers become very productive in the wild, and many will retire themselves away from the city or the telephone to start or finish a book. Plants and greenery is a sure way for your male or female Gemini friend to regenerate. Many have green thumbs and use their inner knowledge of the plants homeopathic values to heal others. Often a body of water is also chosen, as subconsciously, Gemini is aware of the regeneration principle-taking place when walking barefoot on the dirt or by the water. The negative ions found by the water will ground the high Mercurial spirit and make your male or female friend born in June more grounded and much more productive. Virgo rules also natural chemicals and a soul born in June is a natural and gifted photographer. The mixture of chemicals used to process the pictures is often sorted, stored and used from the base of operation in the photography studio. A word of caution: If you are into photography, make sure to dispose of those chemicals carefully and do not inhale the dangerous vapors.

Gemini, House Number 5

Let's now look at how a Gemini behaves or feels about love. So now let's look in House Number 5 for those born in June. In the love area, your male or female Gemini friend becomes a Libra. So now let's look at House Number 5 in the Section Housing System and read the keywords and get more information. Remember you can also refer to the Sun Sign Characteristics and read all about this Sun Sign. In the 5th House of love and romance and children, your friends or acquaintances born in June will attract those born in October or February. This is also the House of Speculations. Libra rules the law. That is why many Gemini's are great attorneys because in their speculation area they are the scale, the scale is balance and harmony, also the opportunity to learn psychology or the more advanced science of Astropsychology. Those born in June are extremely creative with their hands. Remember Gemini rules the hands. Many of them love mechanics and others work in junkyards. Being a Leo in the area of love, romance and children, your male or female friend born in June will behave childlike with love. Many of them, of course, work with children and usually this sign is gifted with photography and drawing. They also love to tell jokes and will not miss any opportunity to enjoy life to the fullest. Because the 5th House is Leo and this sign rules parts of France and Italy, your male or female friend born in June will dream of going to France or learn one of those languages. Libra is the sign of balance and harmony, while Leo is creativity. Thus, as Libra is an intellectual air sign, fire and air mix well and can help your Gemini friend accomplish miracles in the arts. As mentioned earlier, Libra rules the law, balance, harmony, Astropsychology and your friend born in June is simply loaded with creativity.

Mercury rules Gemini, this planet rules also communication, writing, driving, telephones, learning and teaching. Many of these souls are great teachers and as they are in some way childlike themselves, all the kids will love to be around them. They do not ask a child to be more than what he is, and they can adapt to them at any given time. They love the outdoors, sports, and action, and will share it all with all the children of the world.

Gemini, House Number 6

Now let's see how your male or female friend born in June behaves or feels about servicing the world. In the work area, your male or female Gemini friend becomes a powerful Scorpio. Refer to the keywords to understand this House better. Scorpio rules investigation metaphysics, life and death and even working at night. The kingdom of the night, of famous radio host, Art Bell speaks for itself. He is a Gemini, and works all night long. Scorpio rules anything and everything to do with investigations, and anything and everything to do with science and metaphysics. Now, remember, Gemini is a sign ruled by Mercury, and will drive the soul towards speaking or writing. This sign also rules fast transportation or your local emergency services. The ambulance or fire engine driver is a good example to represent the speed of Gemini, and in some way, the 6th House of work and service to the world. Now your male or female friend born in June becomes a Scorpio and Scorpio rules drama, death, the police force, etc. Thus, servicing a dangerous, even deadly world as a Scorpio, he has to practice CPR and do it fast. Thus, the potential is right there, right now, real fast to bring back life to the victim of a road accident, and do all he can to bring the victim to the emergency room where a single minute can mean life or death. The same applies for the fire engine driver risking his precious life, speeding to save someone else's life. A cameraman/photographer (during war times), who's job it is to bring the pictures back to his countrymen. These are also good illustrations of Gemini's work and service to the world. Because Scorpio is a deadly sign, and this sign rules the police force, statistics have indicated the highest levels of suicides have taken place within the police force. Scorpio also rules ultimate power, the Mafia, sex, and on a very negative path could lead the soul towards an early grave by dealing with criminals or killers. Scorpio is the sign of life and death and indicates the potential for those born in June to regenerate in working in metaphysics, in the medical field, or in a dangerous or deadly environment. In 1996, on my way back from a conference in Phoenix, Arizona, a police officer born in June stopped me for speeding. Knowing that he was a Gemini, I knew he was curious and we struck up a conversation about Astrology. After doing his stars, in the middle of the desert, in the middle of the night, he let me get away with it and thanked me for giving him my book and the information I gave him.

Gemini, House Number 7

So now let's look in House Number 7 for those born in June. In the home area, your male or female Gemini friend becomes a Sagittarius. So now let's look at House Number 7 in the Section Housing System and read the keywords and get more information. Remember you can also refer to the Sun Sign Characteristics and read all about this Sun Sign. On the 7th House of Marriage and Business Partnerships, souls born in June will attract those born in December, or foreigners. It indicates also the potential they were born with to become teachers, philosophers and publishers. They usually travel the world and do well with foreign people, and sometimes end up marrying a foreign person. Do not be fooled, even if he or she talks a lot, your male or female friend born in June is by birth very spiritual. This 7th House is ruled by the biggest planet in our solar system and called in Greek mythology Jupiter, the "Lord of Luck and Expansion." Because Jupiter is an expansive planet, those born in June strive for philosophy and many advanced souls teach others the laws of man or those of the universe. Sagittarius rules also the Indians and animals, especially horses. Those born in June have a natural ability to deal with animals and many will work hard to enforce Indian laws. On the negative aspect, as Jupiter rules the codification of thoughts, books and traditional religious education, many young souls born in June will fall for organized religion and will cruise the world to pass on their specific biblical message. Sagittarius' symbol is half man and half horse. The horse simply represents the constant desire to travel the world. The man, the bow and arrow, represents their constant desire to travel spiritually. The challenge is for them to realize that, what the majority has accepted as true is not necessarily so. So, the soul must aim outside of the books and aim for a much higher level of awareness. Aiming into the Universal Mind without classifying God in a man made building, way of life or doctrine, is a serious challenge to them. Thus, many change religion during the course of their lives. Understanding both the physical and spiritual values of those stars will give them the golden key to understand how God speaks to us, through his ultimate cosmic will.

Gemini, House Number 8

So now let's look in House Number 8 for those born in June. In the area of life and death, legacy, metaphysics and corporate money, your male or female Gemini friend becomes a Capricorn. So now let's look at House Number 8 in the Section Housing System and read the keywords and get more information. Remember you can also refer to the Sun Sign Characteristics and read all about this Sun Sign. Slowly but surely your Gemini friend will build up spiritual knowledge and establish financial security. Because Capricorn rules traditional education, many of your male or female friends born in June will gain recognition by educating themselves. But the world of Capricorn rules also metaphysics, politics and large religious corporations. Thus, as this House rules also managing and distributing other peoples gathered money, many of them will use their inner knowledge to get financial support to fulfill their aims. Souls born in June can and do attract Uncle Sam's financial help, and many will operate within a highly structured environment. Capricorn is very shrewd in business and many Gemini's build financial towers for themselves and those they care for. Many invest in valuable properties or get a well-deserved retirement plan from the government. The goat or Capricorn is also a representation of the head of the devil by religious people. Mainly because of the structuring and building power of Saturn, which is the ruler of Capricorn and is the 8th House of Corporate Money (for those born in June). While religious groups have an inborn fear to expand their mind outside of the past, Gemini questions everything, and will use his resources to build the new future. Capricorn rules also the upper class, structure, career, high achievement, status and metaphysics. Thus, many of your male and female friends born in June will also invest and gain in the homeopathic medical or spiritual fields. During the course of their lives, many will encounter many powerful foreign spiritual figures and will invest time and money to gain more spiritual knowledge. The young Gemini souls may also participate in voluntary endeavors and invest his own money to promote and preach conventional teaching outside of his natal country. Nurturing religious dogmas will not fulfill their aim to teach Universal Love and respect to the children of the world but will classify and separate the spirits. These endeavors ultimately produce religious wars.

Gemini, House Number 9

So now let's look in House Number 9 for those born in June. In the area of traveling, teaching, higher education and foreigners, your male or female Gemini friend becomes an Aquarius. Aquarius means total freedom, traveling the world and the potential to learn and use computers. Many of them will educate themselves in hi-tech, radio, and television. Studying electronics will be rewarding to them, and in the process your male or female friend born in June will gain a good career position. Aquarius rules UFOs, the future, astrology and everything to do with flying. So many Gemini's love to fly, physically or spiritually. Many of them also are masters in handling cameras and photographic equipment. Being so freedom oriented and original in their House of learning, many Gemini will travel far in body, mind and spirit. Many take on studies involving the cosmos, astronomy or Astropsychology. The desire to explore the unconventional and the future is very strong to a Gemini, and some turn themselves into great explorers or inventors. You can be sure that, as Aquarius rules friends, that your male or female friend born in June will have friends all over the world. This Mercury driven spirit likes to travel far and high, and many work for well-established airline companies. Others will follow the Aquarius impulse and may become proficient UFO researchers, speakers or famous writers. Friends born in August and February will be sharing the same desire to explore as your male or female friend born in June. Intellectual stimulation is important for them and the souls born in June will quickly lose interest with those less inquisitive than they are. Gemini needs stimulation, action and mental challenges and many souls born in June will do all they can to avoid a boring daily routine. It is important for Gemini to concentrate and learn to finish any task. Doing so will allow them to reach a position of respect and establish the security their do strive for. As a rule, these souls will regenerate by communicating, traveling, learning and teaching the children of the world.

Gemini, House Number 10

So now let's explore House Number 10 or the area of career and of public standing for those born in June. In that section of life, your male or female Gemini friend becomes a soft Pisces. So now let's look at House Number 10 in the Section Housing System and read the keywords and get more information. Remember you can also refer to the Sun Sign Characteristics and read all about this Sun Sign. Pisces rules the medical field, the subconscious, psychic work, painting, music, dancing, and of course, the oceans. So many people born in June are teachers of the waves and some work for Sea World or Disneyland. They do enjoy a lot of activity, and in the process, they can teach you anything and everything about the world of water or creativity. Music, dancing, skating, painting, acting, cinematography, deal with Poseidon, the Lord of the Waves. Pisces also rules the medical field and many of those born in June have a serious commitment to heal others and many become nurses. Sometimes the desire to provide for others is so strong that many work in raising money or participate in volunteer work. Because Neptune rules photography and Gemini reporting the news, many will also work as reporters for large newspapers or famous magazines. Male or female souls born in June will also have the opportunity to have their photography placed in magazines. Many speakers and promoters of the apocalyptic time will also serve and turn themselves into priests and further a specific organized religious purpose. The desire to help and to be on the move is so strong that many of your male or female friends born in June will travel the world providing help to those in trouble. Because Pisces is a very creative sign, many souls born in June will gain recognition in the arts. Gemini is very creative by birth and their artistic expression is quite phenomenal. Because Pisces is a water sign, it is important for them to educate themselves and avoid daydreaming. Mercury, the ruler of the Printed Word, may also lead many of his children to work in bookstores or large telecommunication industries. Many Gemini's also work on the telephone as counselors or psychics. The worse that can happen is total confusion in choosing a career due to the duality involving this sign. But once educated, your male or female friends born in June can accomplish miracles in a very rewarding career endeavor.

Gemini, House Number 11

So now let's explore House Number 11 and see how your Gemini friends behave with their friends. In that section of life, your male or female Gemini friend becomes an impatient Aries. So now let's look at House Number 11 in the Section Housing System and read the keywords and get more information. Remember you can also refer to the Sun Sign Characteristics and read all about this Sun Sign. In the area of wishes and Friends, those born in June attract and will get their wishes granted with those born in April or Aries. So those born in April and October have the potential to bring Gemini wishes. Aries rules the head, Aries rules the "me" and the "I" which means that once Gemini realizes his dual personality and finds himself, he will be able to reach his wishes. Aries is a very competitive sign, thus, your Gemini friend will strive to get as many friends as he can. But don't expect him or her to stay around for long, as other friends need their help. Your male or female friend born in June loves and needs to talk. As a rule the telephone bill can get real heavy and many lose their account. It is important for you to discipline your Gemini friend and tell him to express himself fast. Many will resent them, as they are so busy with life that they also forget to nurture older friends. Chances are that your Gemini male or female friend will have friends from all over the world, but don't expect them to take the time to sit down and write long letters. The telephone or the Internet is much faster to them. Again the location of the Moon or the Dragon's Head and Tail could intensify or diminish their gift of communication. Mars rules Aries and this sign loves speed and danger. Thus, your male or female friend may decide to become a racing driver, a stuntman or chose to enjoy an element of adventure and danger with his friends. The constant push of Mars in the House of wishes makes your Gemini friends in a hurry to get to their wishes or deal with his friends. You may also encounter a supposed to be slow Taurus born in May behaving this way. That's because he may have inherited a

I Know All About You 75

fast Moon or Dragon in Gemini at birth. Thus, the same applies for anyone born under any sign of the zodiac. The position of the planet Mercury, ruler of Gemini, will also play an important part to the speed and dual personality involving a Gemini.

Gemini, House Number 12

So now let's explore House Number 12 and see how your Gemini friends behave subconsciously. In that section of the human experience, your male or female Gemini friend becomes a solid Taurus. So now let's look at House Number 12 in the Section Housing System and read the keywords and get more information. Remember you can also refer to the Sun Sign Characteristics and read all about this Sun Sign. On the subconscious area someone born in June or a Gemini becomes a Taurus. You may think of your Gemini friend as superficial or unstable but that is not the case. They might also appear to be jack-of-all-trades and get involved in too many projects. But being fast, inquisitive, curious changing and telling a lot of jokes is part of their character. But, don't forget, in the back of their head, in the subconscious level they are Tauruses, and they are motivated by a strong subconscious desire for security and solidity. Taurus rules also the arts and money; thus, your male or female friend born in June might have a subconscious fear not to be able to get enough resources to survive or to be accepted by others as a great artist. This subconscious motivation is so strong and stubborn that your friend born in June will try all he can to achieve both. They do long for a super busy life, make tons of money and finally get a mansion somewhere in an exotic place. Of course any planet in the 12th House will also play an important part of its subconscious motivation. Much more can be divulged especially in my book *The Power of the Dragon*. Because the subconscious is somehow deceiving, your male or female friend born in June may have a conflict between physical possession and spiritual knowledge. It is important for them to realize that there is nothing wrong with money and absolutely nothing wrong in making money with knowledge. That's why many of them service the world for free and get used and abused by religious groups. The gift of communication, the desire for security, the inner desire to help is very real. Many will be able to get the balance, security and knowledge they are striving for.

Astropsychology Profile
Cancer

Let us move on now and explore those born in July. The soul's purpose of your Cancer friend is to explore sensitivity and enjoy security, home, family and food. In many ways, those born in July must feed and protect the world either physically or spiritually. Cancer is also a water sign, and will respond drastically to the Moon's fluctuations.

Cancer, House Number 1

The soul's purpose of your friends born in July is to feed and protect his family and the world at large. The Moon rules Cancer and many souls born in July feed also the world spiritually. Cancer also rules housing, clothing, hotels, restaurants, food, real estate, and all that means security. Mr. Ross Perot was born in July and he is a good example of the good old American dream for the American people. For your information, Cancer rules the United States, as the date of the signing of the Declaration of Independence was July 4, 1776. That is why this country sends planes loaded with food and clothing all over the world when the situation arises. America is like a big fridge, able to feed itself and much of the rest of the world too. On a more amusing note, because of the availability of food, the American people also spend millions of dollars to lose fat. Emotional, sensitive and caring, those born in July are totally under the power of the Moon. It is important for them to initiate all endeavors after the New Moon when their ruler is waxing and avoid depression during the waning Moon. Because Cancer is a water sign living or operating close to the water will always be beneficial to them. To represent food and security, the ancient astrologers carved and painted the crab. The idea behind the symbol of Cancer, the crab is to symbolize food and what does the crab do all day long? He eats! Of course the food supply is the ocean. As the crab walks sideways he cannot really climb the vertical wall of a slippery rock. Thus, as the Moon control the tides, the crab must wait for the next tide to be raised to the top of the rock and enjoy the food deposited by the previous tide. This again indicates why understanding and respecting the Moon's fluctuations is a must for all water signs. Regardless of the month of your birth, every one of us has an area ruled by the Moon in our chart. Consequently, this law does apply to each one of us. Your male or female friend born in July is close to his family and will treat you like his own family too. Those born in July have a great appetite and enjoy not only cooking but also eating. Unless a more health-oriented moon in an earth sign affects your Cancer friend's psyche, many of them often do indulge themselves with too much food and gain weight. Because the crab possesses two powerful claws, your male or female Cancer friend will not let go of you or the past easily. Letting go of the wrong people and the past is part of their lesson.

Cancer, House Number 2

Let's explore the House of money and self-esteem for

those born in July. So now let's look at House Number 2 in the Section Housing System and read the keywords and get more information. Remember you can also refer to the Sun Sign Characteristics and read all about this Sun Sign. Again, millionaire Ross Perot was born in July and in his Second House of Money, he becomes a Leo, as Leo rules love, fame, children and power. Thus your male or female friend born in July has, like Ross Perot, the potential to shine with money. Cancer will show love with money and they will spend a lot on their children. Departed, Princess Diana was born in July and much of her time and money was spent and made to stop the suffering of the children of the world. But the Second House is not all about spending resources it is also about making money. So many people born in July will spend money learning an art so that they can also make plenty of it by performing. Understand that Leo is ruled by the Sun, during the day all planets shy away from the Sun. This means a stage will be used to show off while performing the arts. Actor Bill Cosby was born in July and his family oriented show points out the caring, loving father of the zodiac. Not to forget famous Aquarius TV host Oprah Winfrey born with a Dragon's Tail in Cancer. Many Cancers are great singers, and this sign rules country music. Incidentally, Cancer rules the breasts and many famous singers and actors such a Dolly Parton, Marilyn Monroe and Pamela Anderson were born with a strong Dragon's Head in Cancer. Cancer means home, family and children; thus, many famous TV hosts with a show revolving towards family matters or children will be, or have a strong Cancer in their chart such as Geraldo Rivera, Montel Williams and Jay Thomas. Thus, the potential for them to reach the homes and families of millions of Americans is offered to them thereby gaining fame and fortune. Your male or female friend born in July is a magnet for love and money and if you are lucky enough to know a Cancer treat him/her right, as their luck with money will get to you too. Children, love, security, family, food, the arts, fame, and good fortune will always come to them naturally. You had better take good care of them, as they will in turn take good care of you.

Cancer, House Number 3

The 3rd House, rules the thinking process, thus, your friend born in July becomes a Virgo. So now let's explore this area for those born in July. So now let's look at House Number 3 in the Section Housing System and read the keywords and get more information. Remember you can also refer to the Sun Sign Characteristics and read all about this Sun Sign. Because Virgo is a sign ruled by Mercury, souls born in July will be intellectually inclined. Traditionally, Virgo rules the 6th House or the temple of God, which is your body and especially the digestive track. Virgo cleanses, cleans and organizes. That's why you will find many Cancer's working in office, managerial and clerical positions. Virgo is the sign of health, purity and greenery; thus, chances are that your male or female friend born in July could be overly concerned with health and turn themselves into a vegetarian. The Virgo power on your Cancer friend's mind is very strong and could make them critical, fussy, fault finding and somehow perfectionists. That's OK if this attitude is used at work in dealing with paper work at the office. But if directed against others or himself, your friend could seriously suffer and turn the thinking process into health fanaticism. Remember Princess Diana was a victim of many eating disorders and like many other souls born in July, she was the victim of the strong Virgo pull. Many famous actors and actresses born with a strong Virgo in their natal chart will do all they can to look beautiful and pure, and sadly enough many do starve to death. The idea is to remember that the Virgin Mary or the sign of Virgo, works for you! You don't work for her. In that respect you can control your thoughts and actions and be above the subconscious fear of decay or disease. Because Virgo is a health-oriented sign, your male and female friend born in July could be attracted to medicine and do very well in the process. A Taurus born friend of mine was born with his Dragon's Tail in Virgo, and works as a surgeon in a local hospital. If you are a Cancer, control your thought process, nobody is perfect, not even me, not even you, relax.

Cancer, House Number 4

So now let's investigate House Number 4 for those born in July. In the home area, your male or female Cancer friend becomes a Libra. So now let's look at House Number 4 in the Section Housing System and read the keywords and get more information. Remember you can also refer to the Sun Sign Characteristics and read all about this Sun Sign. Because Libra rules balance and harmony, you can be sure that your male or female friend born in July will treat every one of his family members equally. This sign is ruled by Venus, the planet of love, thus, being at peace and loved by everyone is a must for Cancer. Libra rules also the law, and many souls born in July will have to deal with wills and the sharing of their lifetime resources after their death on even terms with all the members of his cherished family. Many important legal activities and contracts are dealt with at home, and many Cancers thrive in the real estate business. The colors, attitude and all that make the home area could hinder, for better or for worse, those born in July. It is important for them to do all they can to bring about love and peace at home. They also have an inner aptitude to do interior designing and mix colors gracefully inside of their home. Because Venus is an artistic sign, many will either listen or make great music at home. Your friend born in July is a natural mediator in dealing with those who visit him and will make anyone feel comfortable and welcome in their home. Sometimes, in order to bring about the balance and harmony they strive for, your male or female friend born in July will compromise to save trouble and bring about the peace of Libra. In that respect many of those loving souls get used and abused by their own children. Thus, Cancer must realize their weak side and become less emotional with the children. Standing firm with the family resources is a must and sharing all equally is part of their desire. Because Cancer is a Moon ruled sign, they all must be aware of the Moon's fluctuations when signing important contracts. The important paperwork must be signed after the New Moon to avoid future problems. After the Full Moon, especially a few days before the New Moon, your male or female Cancer friend might become a bit moody or depressed or very sensitive to family problems. Help them to deal with it by surrounding them with love and happiness.

Cancer, House Number 5

Let's now look at how a Cancer behaves or feels about love, romance and children. So now let's look at House Number 5 in the Section Housing System and read the keywords and get more information. Remember you can also refer to the Sun Sign Characteristics and read all about this Sun Sign. In the love area, your male or female Cancer friend becomes a very intense Scorpio. In the 5th

House of love and romance and children, your friends or acquaintances born in July will attract those born in November or March. Pluto rules Scorpio and this planet is extremely intense and climactic. Thus, those born in July might have to experience drama in the affairs of love, romance and children. Because Scorpio is the sign of life and death, your male or female friend born in July might have had a dramatic upbringing, lost a child, or suffered dramatic heartaches. Wherever Scorpio's House or Pluto is located in a chart, a regeneration principle is offered to the soul; thus, Cancer regenerates with the children, with love and romance. Scorpio is also a very metaphysically oriented sign. Thus, your male or female friend born in July is a born investigator of Astropsychology, astrology, metaphysics, psychic work and all matters related to life and death. A large portion of my best students and clients are born in July. As seen with Princess Diana's work, Cancer will always regenerate by involving himself with children, as did Mother Teresa a Leo or the sign ruling love, light and children. This also indicates why Princess Diana was inquisitive of the future and dealt with astrologers and psychics. Scorpio rules death and drama, thus, your male and female friend, like Princess Diana has been given the potential to bring life and relief where the children of this world experience death and suffering. In the affairs of love, Scorpio is a very passionate, sensual sign and so is your male and female friend born in July. This is the area of speculation and indicates Pamela Anderson's incredible sexual and love appeal. Scorpio too is a deadly sign, and the fatal Scorpion stinger of death and drama generated the O.J. Simpson dilemma.

Cancer, House Number 6

Look at House Number 6 to see and realize how your male

or female friend born in July behaves or feels about health and servicing the world. In the work area, your male or female Cancer friend becomes a Sagittarius. So now let's look at House Number 6 in the Section Housing System and read the keywords and get more information. Remember, you can also refer to the Sun Sign Characteristics and read all about this Sun Sign. By birth, your male or female friend born in July becomes a philosopher. Sagittarius rules also animals and many Cancers will invest time and money to alleviate animal suffering. Many of them are also very caring and precise veterinarians. Sagittarius also rules horses and the Indian's world, thus they can also operate and work in these areas. Given a choice, your Cancer friend will aim for homeopathic medicine, as intuitively he or she is aware of the damage inflicted by all prescription side effects. On the physical medical aspect of Astropsychology, Sagittarius rules the back or the connection between the man and the horse. Thus, backache is common especially if overweight. Cancer is a water element and this lunar sign tend to retain liquid in their tissues. Lots of activity and the sauna would help to get rid of the surplus weight. Sagittarius rules also the codification of thought and the law. Many successful Cancers are blessed with an understanding of both man and God's laws. Thus, they can turn into effective attorneys or philosophers. Sagittarius rules also publishing foreign lands and religion. Thus, your male or female friend born in July will spend money traveling and educating themselves in foreign philosophy. Fresh air and spending time in the wild is also very beneficial for these souls. They also tend to regenerate with animals and many own dogs, cats, horses, and birds. Being one with nature and protecting the wildlife is part of their desire to feed and protect mother earth. Many are great teachers and will service the world by educating the children. Children are attracted to those born in July mostly because they can subconsciously sense a strong and pure desire to protect and feed. Their natural positive attitude and faith will protect their body for a long time and make those born in July one of the longest living signs of the zodiac.

Cancer, House Number 7

So now let's look in House Number 7 for those born in July and see how and with whom your male or female friend born in July faces the world. In the partnership area, your friend becomes a Capricorn. So now let's look at House Number 7 in the Section Housing System and read the keywords and get more information. Remember you can also refer to the Sun Sign Characteristics and read all about this Sun Sign. On the 7th House of Marriage and business partnerships, souls born in July will attract those born in November and March. Capricorn is the sign of honor, accomplishments and career. Thus, your Cancer friend will not mingle with people who have nothing to offer. They are looking for people who have talent, title, education or those who can take care of them and the ever so important family. In that respect, your friend born in July will attract older people when young and much younger as they get older. Capricorn, in some way is a snob or a person who is respected in the community. Your male or female Cancer friend will not settle for less. However, if he or she detects any potential for success and security, he or she will work really hard to bring about the best of the partner. After many years of hard work, many Cancer souls will gain a position of power, authority and success. Some also decide to work for large corporations, Uncle Sam, or simply build a pyramid of success for themselves. Capricorn is a very shrewd business oriented sign and many Cancers end up meeting and marrying the most powerful man in the company. In the marriage area, Saturn, the ruler of Capricorn, will induce a lot of challenges and some times Cancers do marry a very successful person late in life. Your emotional, sensitive Cancer friend turns out to be cold, calculated, smart and decisive when facing the world or in choosing a marriage partner. Subconsciously, your male or female friend born in July is looking for a good mother or a strong father for the children, withstanding it all for the well being of the family. Security, food, and family mean a lot to Cancer; and unless the partner has been tested and has domestic power, there is no chance for business or emotional commitment. Cancer needs a solid family and lots of security.

Cancer, House Number 8

Let's see what going on in House Number 8 for those born in July. In the area of life and death, legacy, metaphysics and corporate money, your male or female Cancer friend becomes an Aquarius. So now let's look at House Number 8 in the Section Housing System and read the keywords and get more information. Remember you can also refer to the Sun Sign Characteristics and read all about this Sun Sign. In some ways Cancer will always be interested in the after-life and affairs of the dead. This House deals with legacy and Cancer is very conscious of what will happen to his family after his departure from this world. Thus, much work will be done to make sure his valuable possessions are shared equally to the members of his family. Aquarius is the sign that rules astrology, thus, your male or female friend born in July will explore the old science thoughtfully. It often indicates that the soul has many times, in previous incarnations learned about

I Know All About You

his direct relationship with the Universal Mind and the stars above. Cancer is quite intuitive by birth and expanding their knowledge of the heavens can only help them to synchronize harmoniously with the stars. This House also rules the money coming from a business and many Cancer students of mine graduated in Astropsychology and are making good money and good use of this rare knowledge. Aquarius rules also electronics; the stock market and many souls born in July are adept in corporate money and are attracted to many investment endeavors. Much money will be gained or lost based upon their awareness of the timing involving the Universal Laws. The most important one of course is coming from their ruler, the Moon. It is important for them to realize the importance of promoting all that they touch after the New Moon; and to use the waning period of the Moon to make plans or finish what has been started. Accordingly, my yearly publication **Moon Power** is a serious guide to them. Regardless of the month of your birth, this law will touch every one of us, as we all have a Moon sign. The Moon will be felt especially in the affairs involving all water areas of your chart. Cancer is very emotional in nature and as Aquarius rules friends, when an acquaintance is lost; the pain experienced is quite deep. Cancers are not afraid to help their friends and many of them have long-standing friends involved in their moneymaking schemes. Aquarius loves to travel both the physical and spiritual worlds; thus, your male or female friend born in July will spend money doing just that.

Cancer, House Number 9

How does your Cancer friend feel or behave in House Number 9? This is the area of religion, traveling, learning, teaching, publishing and relationships with foreigners. In this area your male or female Cancer friend becomes a Pisces. So now let's look at House Number 9 in the Section Housing System and read the keywords and get more information. Remember you can also refer to the Sun Sign Characteristics and read all about this Sun Sign. Pisces is ruled by Neptune, or in Greek mythology Poseidon, the Lord of the Seas. Cancer loves, water, cruising on a ship, or spending time in exotic places. Understand that Pisces is the sign subconsciously chosen by Christianity to represent feelings and religion. On the negative aspect, "Poseidon" is also deceiving and could lure your Cancer friend into impractical or deceiving "Neptunian" people or endeavors. Being a water sign Pisces has no grounding and tends to deal with this area of life with imagination or guilt. Their deep feeling for life and natural orientation to care for others does appeal to the manipulators. Thus, this traditional sign is also prone to get used and abused by organized religion. Much of their resources are sometimes left to promote dogmas in the classification of God through their birth or newfound religion. The more advanced souls invest in the true light for the children of tomorrow by furthering Universal Knowledge and Universal Love. Many people born in July are natural psychics and many do very well in helping others spiritually. Because the 9th House rules foreigners and foreign cultures, many Cancers will invest and travel far in search of the truth, not knowing that the answers they are so desperately looking for has always been right above their head, in the stars. Parts of the Bible mentioning, "And God created the stars and the heavens" and that "Man was created in the image of God" and "Ask and you shall receive" should be understood and practiced rationally. Regardless of their deep inner desire for religious involvement, your male or female friend born in July is a truly remarkable soul loaded with love and attention for others. Pisces rules also the arts, music, dancing and those born in July are naturally attracted to learn and teach the arts to children. Sometimes their life ends peacefully, close to those they love in an exotic place. Many were born to find the light, master the light and pass on the light to the world through their publishing purpose.

Cancer, House Number 10

Let's now get into House Number 10. This is the area of career, public standing, and accomplishments. In this area your male or female Cancer friend becomes a very competitive Aries. So now let's look at House Number 10 in the Section Housing System and read the keywords and get more information. Remember you can also refer to the Sun Sign Characteristics and read all about this Sun Sign. Mars or "The Lord of War" in Greek mythology rules Aries. Thus your male or female Cancer friend has been given the opportunity to become a leader in his career. Mars means also hazard, explosions, and the power of destruction; thus, Cancer is also attracted to the Navy, the Army or any endeavor involving fire, danger, and competitiveness. Chances are that your local firefighter or the boss of a large and successful company was born in July. In the medical aspect of astrology, Aries rules the head and your Cancer friend might be prone to headaches or head injury. However, this sign is always aware of his commitment to the country and his family and will do all he can to avoid unnecessary risks. Your male or female friend born in July loves to parade for a cause he feels is right and many will lead the march for respect and approval. No matter how sensitive you think Cancer is, when it comes to his career he can be quite determined to succeed. Aries rules the head and this sign will not compromise for anybody and must be recognized by all as the leader. A good representation of the strength, fire, danger and competitiveness of Cancer is well represented by O.J. Simpson's violent career in and out of the football stadium. Tom Cruise and Danny Glover were also born in July and their acting character speaks millions about their roles and career induced by the stars, especially in the "Top Gun" and "Lethal Weapon" movies. If there is one area of life that your male or female friend born in July may beat you, that is in their career accomplishments. So do not fall for modern astrology teachings and think that Cancer is a weak sign.

Cancer, House Number 11

How does your male or female friend born in July feel about friends? So now let's look at House Number 11 in the Section Housing System and read the keywords and get more information. Remember you can also refer to the Sun Sign Characteristics and read all about this Sun Sign. This is the area of wishes, friends, and group organizations. In this area Cancer becomes a solid Taurus. Venus or "The Goddess of Love" in Greek mythology rules this House, and the sign of Taurus. Knowing that Taurus rules money, your male or female friend born in July will surely attract wealthy friends. Sometimes Cancer's involve their close friends in their business ventures. Taurus is the sign of money, so we can also say that Cancer loves to make money and spend money with their friends. This House rules also wishes, and Cancer has a serious desire to make plenty of money. Taurus is a possessive sign; thus, your male or female friend will be reluctant to let go of close friends, and when they lose one, they feel really sad. They can also become too possessive with those they care for. Venus rules Taurus, and the planet Venus is always involved with the arts. Thus, Cancer will spend money on very expensive items. Cancer's love antiques, and they know the value of all they wish to acquire. Cancer friends own well-established businesses, and your male or female friend born in July would also enjoy your hospitality. It is part of their inclination to treat you super well, just to reward you for being such a good friend. Taurus is an earth sign; thus, spending money on expensive rare rocks or diamonds is part of a Cancer craving. Taurus rules also massage and spas. Thus, a good massage followed with good food and candlelight is always a possibility. Taurus rules banking and also Switzerland, and part of your Cancer friend's private wish is to own a secret fat bank account in this country. As always, Venus rules music and singing and many souls born in July own a grand piano, and proudly display the valuable instrument in their home. Those born in May, November and March will be the first choice for a Cancer, and many will revolve around them. Ultimately, as Taurus rules money and Venus love, your male or female Cancer friend has a solid wish to gain and receive all of the best that life and their friends can provide. Always remember to treat them right, because much of their money and real feelings will be offered unselfishly to those great friends.

Cancer, House Number 12

Let's now investigate what going on in the subconscious area of your male or female friend born in July. So now let's look at House Number 12 in the Section Housing System and read the keywords and get more information. Remember you can also refer to the Sun Sign Characteristics and read all about this Sun Sign. This is the area of fear, imagination, the subconscious and deception. In this area Cancer becomes a witty Gemini. Gemini loves to talk, but the subconscious is a private area. Thus, it is important for those born in July to learn to keep any and all secrets, especially when friends and family are concerned. Souls born in July will talk a lot to themselves too. The idea is to make sure that they do communicate with themselves positively. Gemini rules also brothers and sisters and much interest goes in that direction. Being so emotional and family oriented by nature, any mishap with a sibling could alter a Cancerian for life. Pisces traditionally rules the 12th House, and because this sign could be deceiving, it is important for them to control their imagination and the guilt of the past. Gemini is also controlled by Mercury; the planet of communication, writing, speaking, etc. Many Cancers have made good use of their subconscious imaginative powers and have become very famous writers. Others share their talent to the world by singing or writing beautiful music. Because Gemini loves photography, your male or female friend born in July will take plenty of pictures to remind themselves of the good times they had. Because this sign retains water they do tend to feel sad about themselves. They also go back in time with those pictures and look at their young and beautiful body. They must understand that beauty is not only physical but also spiritual, and looking at those young svelte bodies in magazines should not upset them. Many also cry in secret by looking at the pictures in revisiting their past. It is important for them to realize also how the waning moon can negatively affect their subconscious and make them feel depressed. Unlike their physical appearance, their loving, incredible beautiful spiritual nature will never fade away.

Astropsychology Profile
Leo

Okay, we are now ready to explore those born in August. The Sun, ruler of Leo, gives your friends born in August the opportunity to find the light, explore the light, and promote the light. Leo is a fire sign and must learn to use the creative forces of the Sun constructively.

Leo, House Number 1

The soul's purpose of your friends born in August is to shine and make an impact in the world at large. The Sun rules Leo and many souls born in August must understand the importance of running the show. Leo also rules love, romance, children, the stage, fame and life in general. Each and every planet in our solar system is both positive and negative, so are all the Sun Signs. The downfall of this shining sign is to misuse the forces of the Sun and let the ego take over. During the day, all the planets shy away, only the Sun shines and overrides them all. No one can survive without the creative forces of the Sun, everything in this world, plants, animals, sea creatures, and humans, we all need its daily warmth to stay alive. However, in the middle of the dry and harsh desert, the sun's rays are much too strong and burn everything under its jurisdiction and the Sun becomes a killer. It is important for those born in August not to become overbearing, too bossy or self centered. Not all Leo's will behave this way though; a wise Moon or Dragon's Tail in the disciplined sign of Capricorn or shy Pisces will always tone down the power of the King of the zodiac. This sign rules children and the arts, thus Leo is a true magnet to children and will help them to reach the best of their potential. The Sun has given your male or female friend born in August the power to shine, to lead, to create and to reach fame during the course of this reincarnation. The Sun does not really care what you choose to do on this earth, even if you decide to become a nun, like Mother Teresa born in August. Induced by the Sun at birth, she was set to gain fame and eternal recognition for all the good that she did for the children of the world. Some other famous people born in August are Madonna, Michael Jackson, the Queen Mother, Magic Johnson, Napoleon, Princess Anne, Princess Margaret, Jackie Onassis and Robert De Niro. Incidentally, Princess Diana was born in July but her natal Dragon's Head was in the sign of Leo and she spent most of her famous life helping the children. She was born to be a Princess and she behaved like a princess by giving her heart entirely for the children of many foreign nations.

Leo, House Number 2

Let's now explore the House of money and self-esteem for those born in August. So now let's look at House Number 2 in the Section Housing System and read the keywords and get more information. Remember you can also refer to the Sun Sign Characteristics and read all about this Sun Sign. In dealing with money, your male or female friend born in August will be very precise. Remember Virgo rules health, detail, and perfection. Thus, Leo will not sign anything without looking at all the fine lines. Because Leo rules life, your male or female friend born in August might also have a subconscious fear of decay or death; thus, many spend money on their health. Virgo rules plants, and homeopathic medicine; and Leo will invest in herbal products and will swallow many pills to stay young and healthy forever. The shy Leo may also work in a financial office doing paper work and organize others. The more intellectually inclined Leo will also operate in the legal field where organization and investigation play an important part to win a case. Many successful teachers and writers were also born in August and much of their endeavors are directed towards educating the children. I know a beautiful retired teacher born in March with a Dragon's Head in Leo; she spent her entire life doing paperwork and teaching first grade children. The powerful Leo, driven by this House of Health, may also invest much of his time and resources in medical studies and become a doctor. Being a fixed fire sign, chances are your male or female friend born in August will persist and gain notoriety in anything he or she decides to accomplish. You will find a Leo in every walk of life, many of them work in exercise and fitness establishments and use lots of health equipment. Promoting physical life and spiritual health is part of their soul's purpose and your Leo male or female friend enjoys doing so. When the subconscious fear of decay is too strong, problems arises when your Leo friend begins to exaggerate this behavior or tries to impose its rigid rules on others. Being a perfectionist Virgo in the Second House of money and self-esteem, your male or female friend born in August is simply very committed to offer the best to society. Because Leo is the "King" of the zodiac, they usually become leaders in this field. They own and operate many public places where love, light, the arts, and life are offered to all.

Leo, House Number 3

The 3rd House, rules the thinking process, thus, your friend born in August becomes a Libra. So now let's look at House Number 3 in the Section Housing System and read the keywords and get more information. Remember you can also refer to the Sun Sign Characteristics and read all about this Sun Sign. Knowing that Libra rules balance and harmony, it is natural for them to act diplomatically in dealing with others. Libra is also representing the scale of justice; thus, your male or female friend born in August will be attracted to the law or even psychology. Note that President Clinton (a Leo), is also an attorney. It is important for them to realize the importance of educating themselves on both sides of the scale. This means traditional or religious education and in a totally opposite direction such as learning metaphysics and understanding Astropsychology. In that respect both sides of the scale now have information, which will allow your Leo friend to gain balance and harmony by mastering both the physical and spiritual laws. The mind of a Leo is always concerned with love, light, and children and keeping harmony with others in all they say is a part of their communicative gift. This is also a sure recipe for success, especially if the soul operates in the public arena or on the radio. Because Libra rules partners and group organizations, your male or female friend born in August will invest his physical or spiritual artistic talent in others. The desire for harmony is so strong that Leo will compromise in dealing with headstrong souls. However, don't forget that you are still dealing with a Lion here, be sure to play the game fairly for if you don't you could easily end up as a tasty pray. Leo's sense of organization is phenomenal, they know intuitively who has what and how much to offer. If a person born in August has you as a good fiend, you probably passed the hardest test a person can inflict upon another. Thus, you should be proud, as Leo really knows you and your gifts. He will slowly but surely show you what fame, power, and love, are all about.

Leo, House Number 4

So now let's investigate House Number 4 for those born in August. In the home area, your male or female Leo friend becomes a secretive Scorpio. So now let's look at House Number 4 in the Section Housing System and read the keywords and get more information. Remember you can also refer to the Sun Sign Characteristics and read all about this Sun Sign. Because Scorpio rules metaphysical investigation, your male or female friend born in August will have his private den where other family members will have to stay clear and respect his privacy. Pluto, the planet of drama and death, rules Scorpio. Thus, many young Lions, as seen in the wild, experience drama and sometimes an early death. Sadly enough "The Little Queen" of the Ramsey family was born in August and met with her deadly fate on Christmas night. On a more positive side, it is at home where an opportunity to learn important mystical studies such as life and death is offered to the soul. Scorpio rules also sex, and as seen with President Clinton, his home (in this case the White House) became the foreground for sexual activity in the Oval Office, with a young intern named Monica Lewinsky. Your male or female friend born in August needs total privacy at home where he or she can re-birth into the "Eagle" of the zodiac. The sign of Scorpio rules ultimate power, the Mafia, and the police force. Thus, the young Lion's soul, driven by pride, power, and control, could solicit the lowest and deadly elements of society in his home. Plans are made in secret to swiftly eliminate the competition, which ultimately brings the police at the source of the conflict. For protection and privacy purposes, many famous Leo's barricade themselves in their home where the ignorant, psychotic and jealous masses cannot reach or hurt them and their cherished family. Usually, the universe brings them a home of luxury where power, fame and money is used to bring forth the light to others. Intense and spiritual your Leo friends will use the Plutonic power to further acknowledge the rest of the family. This, in time can bring friction with Neptunian acquaintances that tend to follow a more traditional and restrained route to ultimate wisdom.

Leo, House Number 5

Let's now look how a Leo behaves or feels about love, romance and children. So now let's look at House Number 5 in the Section Housing System and read the keywords and get more information. In the love area, your male or female Leo friend becomes a Sagittarius. In the 5th House of love and romance and children, your friends or acquaintances born in August will attract foreigners and those born in February, April and December. Jupiter, the Lord of learning and teaching rules Sagittarius; thus, your Leo friends will strive for knowledge and wisdom. Jupiter rules also animals, horses, dogs, cats, etc., and many Leo souls evolve in the stage arena, while others become proficient trainers or veterinarians. Those born in August will travel far and are fast to expand their spiritual horizons. Incidentally, France and Italy are Leo countries and many Leos will have to dwell with those countrymen. Jupiter rules also publishing, promoting, foreign lands and many Lions will get involved in passing on the philosophical values of Sagittarius. Many young Leo souls will also fall for the codification of thoughts and organized religions. They will tour the world as crusaders of doctrines blinded away from their real purpose. The more advanced souls will perceive, master, and promote the true Universal Light, that he or she is supposed to master, and then pass it on successfully to the rest of the world. When dealing with love, your male or female Leo friend needs a very spiritual partner that can stimulate their powerful solar mind. The passion and the flames of love are intensified day after day if both parties involved are intellectually inclined and in a mission of truth. Many Leo's succeed in their mission as speakers, teachers, and writers. Fame and the stage come naturally to the Lion and the advanced soul is not afraid to share the light with the right partner. Honest, warm, loyal and loving, your Leo male or female friend has the best love to offer to his special mate and the world at large. The powerful light of their ruler; the Sun belongs to them, and they do strive to pass it on to all.

Leo, House Number 6

Let's see how your male or female friend born in August behaves or feels about health and servicing the world. In the work area, your male or female Leo friend becomes a steady Capricorn. So now let's look at House Number 6 in the Section Housing System and read the keywords and get more information. By birth, your male or female friend born in August becomes an engineer of well-planned actions. Capricorn rules also the government and engineering. Many Leo's, as seen with President Clinton, will invest much time to gain recognition in politics, while others sit at the top of their chosen career. Against all odds, like the goat, the soul must climb the highest and treacherous mountain of success.

Nothing will be given to the soul, but Saturn, ruler of Capricorn, always rewards those who work hard. Capricorn will invest time and money to alleviate man's suffering by structuring all that he touches. This House deals well also with health, and while Capricorn is the longest living sign of the zodiac, Leo lives a long and productive life too. Capricorn rules the knees and Leo the back, thus, if you were born in August do not put stress on theses areas. Leo rules life and the young soul may suffer a subconscious fear of death and decay and ingest all sorts of health products or run too much to counteract the inner fear. Many of them gain the position they deserve in sports or academic endeavors. Leo is a fixed sign; thus, regardless of what life throws at them, they possess a will of steel. Like its counterpart sign, Aquarius, Leo was born with all the tools to succeed in life. Wherever the Lion is located in your chart, the opportunity to shine, to run your show and to promote life and light is given to you. The steadiness and planning power of Capricorn is melting into the Leo power making it impossible to fail once a direction has been chosen by the soul. Capricorn rules England while Leo rules France and Italy, thus, your male or female friend born in August may have to travel in those countries or dwell with the people born there. Steady like the Goat, powerful like a Lion, the stars will always promote a soul born in August. Leo's soul purpose is to master and promote the light, while Capricorn will structure and promote the soul right on top of the mountain of success. Dr. Byron Buttler in ("Who's Who in America") is a surgeon and a good Leo friend of mine. He spent his life promoting life and gained the highest respect in the medical community.

Leo, House Number 7

So now let's look in House Number 7 for those born in August and see how and with whom your male or female friend born in August faces the world. So now let's look at House Number 7 in the Section Housing System and read the keywords and get more information. In the partnership area, your friend becomes an inquisitive Aquarius. On the 7th House of Marriage and business partnerships, souls born in August will attract those born in February. Aquarius is an intellectual, original and advanced air sign. This sign rules astrology, Astropsychology, computers, television, the new age and UFOs, etc. Thus, your male or female friend born in August will attract those unique partners. The advanced ones will not mingle with people who have nothing special or advanced to offer. They are looking for people who are original and have special talents. Title, education and money will play an important part of their choice, but as a rule they will choose the mind over money mostly because Leo knows that money can always be made with special talents. Your Leo friend will work hard to find the right partner and they usually succeed. Listening to their head instead of their big heart is always recommended, as Leo is very passionate in the affairs of love. Leo and his chosen unique partner will travel the world and further the world of Aquarius for the well being of humanity. The world will see this couple as unique, extremely magnetic with a very special message to pass on. The young Leo soul will try all he can to attract attention and may favor an erratic hair color, eccentric clothing or pierce his entire body. Because Aquarius is born a rebel, a young Leo soul may support or join a weird group activity and behave eccentrically in public. On a more advanced purpose Leo will always invest time and money to further freedom and knowledge. The need for emancipation is often experienced in flying and by traveling the world. Aquarius rules also television and many successful Lions also work in the public eye. Because Japan is an Aquarius country, many Leo's will experience dealing or traveling this part of the world. As Aquarius rules friends, a close and spiritual friend often introduces the partner.

Leo, House Number 8

Let's see what going on in House Number 8 for those born in August. In the area of life and death, legacy, metaphysics sex and corporate money, your male or female Leo friend becomes a dreamy Pisces. Refer to the Section Housing System and read the keywords to understand this House or this sign better. Leo will always be interested in the after-life and affairs of the dead. Because this sign rules children many give away large amounts of money while alive and after-death. This House deals with legacy and Leo is very conscious of what will happen to his family or the children of the world after his demise. Thus, much work will be done to make sure his valuable possessions are shared equally to the members of his family. Sadly enough the young Leo soul becomes also an easy target for abusive religious groups and all of his life resources are usually given away to further the dogma. Mother Teresa (a Leo) spent all of her valuable life healing and helping others, and the Vatican secretively managed the tremendous wealth she generated to further their own agenda. Pisces rules religion and naturally Leo is the sign of life and usually fears death and the after-life. The research for the spirit is quite strong, and based upon the early religious poisoning, many a fortunes has been wasted to further a chosen religious doctrine. The advanced Leo soul is well aware of the spiritual manipulation involving organized religion and invests in the true light, via the stars. Your male or female friend is quite intuitive by birth and expanding their knowledge of the heaven early enough can only help to make the right investment and further mankind to synchronize harmoniously with the stars. Pisces is a dreamy and religious sign and has no such grounding; thus, imagination and fear blur the soul's judgment in his investment. This is also the House of death, indicating a final resting place close to the water or in an exotic place where the Lion can enjoy the last days of his productive life. On a negative note, Pisces rules also chemicals; drugs, hospitals, mental institutions, and many Leo's end up suffering with Parkinson's disease. Being a soft Pisces in the corporate area is a blessing as long as the resources are used to help others to face life's challenges. Being an impractical Pisces in this House can only help abusive religious organizations to gain more power; and poison more minds to pick their specific God, their specific church, their specific way of life, and/or their specific doctrine. Doing so takes away the Universal Love and ultimate celestial rules written by God in the stars.

Leo, House Number 9

How does your Leo friend feel or behave in House Number 9? So now let's look at House Number 9 in the Section Housing System and read the keywords and get more information. This is the area of religion, traveling, learning, teaching, publishing and relationships with foreigners. In this area your male or female Leo friend becomes an Aries. Aries rules the head and this sign is ruled by Mars, or in Greek mythology "The Lord of War." As Aries rules the mind and the self, Leo must find himself first then use the creative forces of the Sun to further the light upon the world. In this Aries warlike House, many young Leo souls are crusaders and sail the world imposing aggressively their views of the truth upon others. This attitude usually transforms the soul into a preacher of a specific organized religion. The advanced Leo knows better and educates himself independently outside of the regular imposed belief system. Once the independent self and the celestial truth are reached, Leo is then given the opportunity to become a leader in the House of teaching and publishing. Leo can easily reach the masses in this House and must pass on his knowledge without spiritual pride. Aries is extremely independent and rules the discovery principle, thus, if your Leo friend is part of any group, chances are the truth he is promoting is not his own but enforced in his psyche at an early age. On a physical level, Aries rules also engineering, violent sports, speed, danger, fire, exploration and competitiveness. Thus, many famous Leo's have reached the best of their physical expression and shine on stage, in the ring or in the field. The advanced Leo souls may decide to reach the best of the spiritual Aries side and further the awareness and the mind of mankind. Understand also that I translate the laws of the Universe with my own celestial gift, I don't write the laws. This is not a direct attack on religion or any specific group. Regardless of your feelings or celestial direction, the laws as I perceive them are the laws written in light. And in my world, God never came down and wrote no books, but he made the stars so that, in exploring them, you can live a more productive life.

Leo, House Number 10

Let's now get into House Number 10. This is the area of career, public standing and accomplishments. In this area your male or female Leo friend becomes a very steady Taurus. Refer to the Section Housing System and read more to understand this House or this sign better. Venus, "The Queen of Love" in Greek mythology rules Taurus. Thus, your male or female Leo friend has been given the opportunity to deal with the art, money, and establish a strong career. Taurus rules the throat, music, and singing. Madonna and Michael Jackson were both born in August and both reflect the artistic values generated by this sign in this particular House. Leo rules gold and Taurus means money, thus, Leo also invests in prospecting the products of the earth, gold even oil. Incidentally, my good Leo friend, Dr. Butler is also a well-educated geologist and owns an incredible selection of rare gems. Leo is also attracted to the banking industry, geology, gemology, and massage therapy. Chances are that your local bank manager or the CEO of a large and successful financial company was born in August. Any chosen career will always pay off for Leo as long as the physical or spiritual light, beauty, money, the art or the earth is involved. Many of your friends born in August will also thrive in fashion, cosmetics, hairdressing, make-up artistry, or simply be right on stage where they belong. Leo will also find it difficult to give up a career, as Taurus is quite stubborn; but if the situation gets worse, your Leo friend has plenty of will in store to rebuild it even stronger. Many are at the top of the best businesses in town or are simply in the process of building their own kingdom and wealth. Many of my good Leo friends are also surgeons, physicians and practice constructive surgery and help women to be at their best. Leo aims and furthers the physical or spiritual beauty and values of his fellow human beings. In the process, the highly sophisticated or responsible work is rewarded with a well deserved, above average salary. The stubbornness of Taurus is well applied in the pursuit of honor, accomplishment and wealth in the chart of those born under Leo, the king.

Leo, House Number 11

How does your male or female friend born in August feel about friends? Let's simply look into House Number 11 to find out in the Section Housing System for more information. This is the area of wishes, friends and group organization. In this area Leo becomes a witty Gemini. Mercury (Messenger of the Gods) in Greek mythology, rules the sign of Gemini. Knowing that Gemini loves to communicate, much time will be spent with friends on the telephone, getting and passing on the news. Gemini rules radio, books, magazines; and your male or female friend born in August has a wish for education and writing. Sometimes the powerful Lion will involve a close friend in his or her own business venture. This House rules also wishes and your Leo friend has a serious desire to make plenty of money passing out information or being the centerfold of a magazine. Gemini is not a possessive sign, thus, your male or female friend will be a like a butterfly and gain more and more friends in his life. Being so magnetic and attractive, your male or female Leo friend will be reluctant to dwell with possessiveness or jealousy from their friends. They are direct, loving, caring and will feel a real sadness if they lose your friendship. Friends bring their deepest wishes and often love is introduced to them this way. Gemini rules brothers and sisters, thus, wishes can also be reached with them, however; competition with a sibling could bring about stress and conflict. Leo is a fixed sign, but in the friends House they can adapt to anyone and gather the information they need to further their purpose. Many will travel far with a business or emotional partner. The deep wish of your male or female friend born in August is to gather as much information as possible then pass it on to the world in the form of writing or speaking. Gemini rules the radio world, and as seen with President Clinton (a Leo), his daily broadcast to the nation furthers his wish to reach the American people and pass on his valuable information. Incidentally, President Clinton was born with his natal Dragon's Head in Gemini, giving him speech dexterity and his famous dual personality. Communication is a must with Leo. They must guard against speaking too much and keep important secrets to themselves.

Leo, House Number 12

Let's now investigate what going on in the subconscious area of your male or female friend born in August. Look at House Number 12 in the Section Housing System for more information. This is the area of fear, imagination, the subconscious and deception. In this House Leo becomes a soft and emotional Cancer. The subconscious motivation of your male or female friend born in August is to protect and feed spiritually or physically the world around them. Thus, it is important for those born in August to do so for their family and all the people they do care for. Souls born in August are quite extroverted, but on a subconscious level your Leo friend is shy and easily hurt. Cancer rules also the family, the brothers and sisters, and much of their thoughts and responsibility goes in that direction. Cancer is a very spiritual sign and strives for spiritual (or religious) information and direction. Your Leo friend is quite intuitive and will know almost immediately what's wrong around him. The subconscious desire to love, protect and feed is so strong that it is impossible to resist such a powerful caring energy. Leo's inner motivation is to gain knowledge, power and fame so that he or she can feed and protect the world. The Moon's fluctuations will, in time of a full or waning moon, get to your shining friend's psyche. He or she will retire in the past, cry and deal with a very powerful emotion. However, as the moon moves through the heaven, your male or female Leo friend will emerge as happy, and powerful as before. Such a beautiful subconscious motivation to care for the world and children is a part of the Leo karmic key for success and fame. The depth of the moon's emotional nature combined with the Sun's magical ray is often felt in their expressive acting career making Leo the most dramatically oriented sign of the zodiac. Being in love and successful is part of their inner motivation, so that they can fulfill the deep need to care for others.

Astropsychology Profile
Virgo

Let's now explore those born in September. Mercury, ruler of Virgo gives your friends born in September the opportunity to further purity, organization, work, and health. Virgo is an earth sign and must avoid criticism and being over concerned with health.

Virgo, House Number 1

The soul's purpose of your friends born in September is to aim for organization and perfection in all areas of life. Precise and caring, the advanced Virgo will teach the world to improve health standards and will write or speak about it. So now let's look at House Number 1 in the Section Housing System and read the keywords and get more information. The negative aspect of this sign is to overdo it and impose its rigorous rules onto others. Young souls born in September can also be fault finding, critical, extremely rational even skeptical to anything unproven scientifically. Born to promote health and organize all that they touch is a gift that will improve anyone's life. Many souls born in September work in offices and deal quite well with paperwork. Their keen mind is well suited for exploration and investigations and could lead them to operate in psychology or the legal system. Your male or female friend born in September is an intellectual, and languages or legal translation appeals to them. Virgo is the sign in opposition to Pisces, the symbol subconsciously chosen by Christianity. Thus, Pisces must swim upstream towards "The Virgin Mary" using critical thinking and practicality in all they do in their research for perfection. In extreme cases, the strong pull of the sign of Virgo can lead the soul towards a pious life and produces a nun or a priest. Deceived by Virgo, the young soul would repress sexuality or in the case of a nun, marry a deity or Jesus and reach the puritanical virgin's desire for chastity. On a more rational level, the strong pull of Virgo could also produce a myriad of unfounded fears about sex or health matters. The negative pull of Virgo can be quite funny at times. A good friend of mine, born with an over bearing stellium in Virgo turned their own dog into a vegetarian. Doing so can only shorten the life of her pet, as carnivorous animals are designed by nature to eat raw flesh. On the medical aspect of Astropsychology, Virgo rules the 6th House of Health and particularly the digestive track or the elimination, cleansing principle of the body. Like any other sign of the zodiac an exaggeration of the quality Virgo can be just as detrimental, as the very problem they try so hard to avoid. A well-balanced Virgo will see to it and will keep the "Virgin Mary" in check.

Virgo, House Number 2

So now let's look in the money area for those born in September. So now let's look at House Number 2 in the Section Housing System and read the keywords and get more information. Virgo's 2nd House of money is located in the Sign of Libra. This sign rules the law, Astropsychology, art, group organizations, contracts, and marriage. Many people born in September will have to deal with contracts; some also work with the law. Incidentally, attorneys Marcia Clark and Robert Shapiro of the O.J. Simpson infamous murder trial are Virgos, and their professional endeavor shows the power of dedication and the investigative nature of this sign. You will find Virgo almost anywhere where dedications, detail, organization, research and health are concerned. Others work as public speakers, writers, photographers, translators, etc. The ability they possess to produce a perfect result will make them overwork themselves and drain their batteries. A busy public place or a quiet office is a normal place for a Virgo to operate, especially if research, health or communication is involved. The speed and swift thinking they were born with is the perfect gift needed to perform, talk and service the people around them. Because Libra rules the law and contracts, male or female friends born in September will find themselves involved with large corporations, governmental rules or involved with partnership. They are adept at finding solutions to gather the financial support of others and many Virgos are very successful in their career endeavors. On a negative aspect, the wrong partnership and doomed endeavor could end up in court where the karmic relationship would induce serious stress and headaches to all the parties involved. Understanding and following the Universal Laws or using Astropsychology in their business alliances would prove to be beneficial in the long run. Balance, fairness, solid reward and harmony in their financial endeavors is their aim. As the planet Venus rules Libra, they all possess an artistic touch. Also, many Virgo's do very well in the arts especially in writing and photography.

Virgo, House Number 3

In their 3rd House, ruling the thinking process, your friends born in September become a powerful Scorpio. So now let's look at House Number 3 in the Section Housing System and read the keywords to gather more information. This powerful sign gives your Virgo friend the power to investigate all under the Sun. The power of Pluto (ruler of Scorpio) will also give them an intense gaze or beautiful green or blue magnetic eyes. On a negative note, the sarcasm involving Scorpio will be felt through their speech. Remember that Virgo sees everything and their Plutonic mind won't be afraid to tell you the undiluted truth. Sadly enough for them, the very chance to start a business or emotional relationship can be killed before it even starts with this type of intellectual attitude. The advanced ones keep a strong hold on their tongue and avoid criticizing others openly. Scorpio will always regenerate with metaphysics, investments, science, health, astrology and anything demanding spiritual gymnastics. Thus, your male or female friend born in September inherited a powerful mind and can probe your thoughts, motivations and feelings almost immediately. Virgo must avoid using the poisonous stinger of the Scorpion against others and especially against themselves. Sadly enough, Larry was a close friend of mine and he was born in September. A few years ago, he succumbed to the powerful and destructive Dragon's Tail in Scorpio in his mind, and committed suicide. He was a powerful and a well-established businessman and had it all. Many times I advised him about this deadly celestial affliction but the negative stars got the best of him. Those born in September must realize the incredible potential offered to them and must destroy the stinger of the Scorpion. Instead, through education they

I Know All About You 113

can further their own cosmic consciousness and bring about the Eagle or the Phoenix of the zodiac. The mind is well suited to do absolutely anything and the regeneration principle takes place when one investigates matters related to finances, science, health and metaphysics. The thought process becomes very powerful allowing them to find answers and solutions to almost anything. Once the nefarious dart is removed, Virgo can find peace of mind and happiness in every area of his life.

Virgo, House Number 4

So now let's look in House Number 4 for those born in September. Look at House Number 4 in the Section Housing System and read the keywords and more information. In the home area, your male or female Virgo friend becomes a Sagittarius. This is the sign of the wild and represents the Indians, pets, philosophy, and publishing. Virgo rules plants, herbs and greens in the wild, and of course, the rainforest. In that respect many Virgos will choose to live in a rural area or in the desert. They can also reside in a big city, but their home may look in some way like a portion of the rainforest. Many regenerate with plants and gardening. Virgo means organization, paperwork and classification while Sagittarius means learning, teaching and writing. So your friend born in September needs to have a very organized environment where the opportunity to educate himself or others will induce creativity. Meantime, if a less organized Moon or Dragon afflicts the chart, your Virgo friend is much too busy with business to organize his home life and can still operate in a total mess. Like Gemini, Virgo is a Mercury ruled sign; thus, mental stimulation is a must. The desire to exteriorize and explore is produced by the Sagittarius House cusp and it finds its way out through the use of computers, and will travel the world via the Internet. Many Virgos were raised on a farm very close to nature, consequently, the desire to re-establish nature around them is also quite strong. Many Virgos will suffer in the game of love and find people and the world a rough place to be. Your male or female friend born in September may also find a substitute for love with pets. Sagittarius rules domestic and wild animals; many surround themselves and work also with horses. This sign rules also the codification of thoughts and religion; thus, the pious parents play a very important part of their children's failure in partnerships. The upbringing is usually loaded with religious doctrines reinforcing the puritanical and health values of the "Virgin Mary." These early religious teachings usually generate a variety of hang-ups and can seriously alter the soul's perception of sex as a corrupt thing to do. However, with time and discrimination, the soul frees itself from the early mental pollution and does find balance and harmony with others.

Virgo, House Number 5

Let's move on to the 5th House of love and romance, to see what your Virgo male or female friend becomes when he or she is touched by love. Look at House Number 5 in the Section Housing System and read the keywords. Virgo turns into a practical, rational well-organized Capricorn in this House. Thus, Virgo will attract a Capricorn, a Taurus or another sign of the zodiac that has something to offer emotionally and financially. Like all earth signs they do strive for power and security; this is usually found with older, wiser or established people they are attracted to. They are perfectionists in matters of love and will not get involved with anyone just for the sake of having a relationship. Beauty and health are important to them but they need more from you. They are looking at you under a microscope and will perceive your real potential. Capricorn rules power, status, a solid career, respect, titles and accomplishments. They need to know that their chosen partner is well respected and educated. Why waste time with someone who cannot take care of himself? In their mind they want to build not only love but also a business with you. Once a partner has been picked, your male or female friend born in September, (like the goat) will take the long and arduous mountain and climb all the way up to reach your heart. They are capable of incredible sacrifices and the plan usually works in the long run. Virgo is the sign that regulates health, while Capricorn control status and planning. They want their lovers to be hard workers and responsible, as Virgo rules productivity. In that respect not many people will match their standards, and love is usually established later in life if at all. Virgo is a very critical of the people they choose to be with mostly because of their strong desire for perfection and security. Many have an appreciation for high-class arts such as classical music and dancing on the ice where the hard work produced by both partners on the dangerous ground is a representation of what they need to establish in love. On the negative aspect, the young Virgo soul will manipulate their lovers to reach their goals, however, karmic Saturn will see to it and force the soul into material riches along with depressive loneliness. The advanced soul takes on the challenges imposed by Saturn who ultimately rewards them with true accomplishments, and true love.

Virgo, House Number 6

In the 6th House of work, health, and service; souls born in September become ingenious Aquarius. Look at House Number 6 in the Section Housing System for the keywords. This zodiac sign rules computers, electronics, television, and the New Age. Astropsychology, group organization, traveling the world, and anything futuristic is something that appeals to them. Thus, your male or female friend born in September is original, loaded with great ideas and is humanitarian at heart. The strong Virgo sense of detail combined with the electronic touch makes for great inventors and computer wiz'. Many of them work with the stars and will further homeopathic medicine, as Virgo's inner sense of purity rejects all forms of chemicals. Because Aquarius rules the future, a strong sense of guidance and care is often displayed in their chosen career. This sign is altruistic in nature and a true Virgo will exhibit a strong friendship attitude with co-workers. A well-balanced and peaceful environment at work is a must for those born in September. Under stress, Virgo may develop headaches and sinus problems. Aquarius rules the future and progress, and Virgo must feel that he or she is a part of an important purpose that will alleviate mankind's physical or spiritual suffering. This sign is extremely creative and loves any challenge where detail, organization and originality is concerned. Many souls born in September will fly the world around, as Aquarius rules aeronautics. Some will choose to service the world as pilots, flight attendants, writers, speakers, and doing important business. Virgo means service to the world while Aquarius is the opportunity to reach for the world. When it comes to work, Virgo is totally unselfish and absolutely committed. The high Aquarius inner drive will allow many souls born in September to fulfill their deep need to offer only the best to the world.

Virgo, House Number 7

So now let's look in the House of marriage and see how those born in September deal with the world. In the 7th House of relationships, your male or female Virgo friend becomes a soft loving and emotional Pisces. Look at House Number 7 in the Section Housing System for the keywords. Because Pisces is a totally unselfish sign, many Virgos will attract strong and controlling or deceiving Neptunian partners. Pisces is a water sign and has no such grounding. Thus, geared by emotion and sensitivity, Virgo could be easy pray to a soft-spoken manipulator, and in the process seriously damage their existing relationship. Neptune, the ruler of Pisces rules the Middle East, drugs and alcohol, thus, they could attract deceiving Neptunian's, especially under the influence. Pisces rules the 12th House of hidden matter and ruling the 7th House of marriage, many young souls born in September fall for secretive, deceiving, and clandestine relationships. The acquaintances are usually met on the social scene, introduced by a Neptunian friend or at a bar, as Pisces rules alcohol. The young Virgo soul will attract drug addicts, alcoholics, hence, joining them in the very deep and dangerously deceptive waters of Neptune. Your male or female friend born in September will literally sacrifice himself to save or improve any relationship, and they need to stand strong when enough is enough. The Pisces self-eluding nature may make them feel guilty, shy or undeserving due to a lack of self-esteem in dealing with the world and others. On a more positive note, the advanced Virgo soul has no problem to offer true love, respect and sacrifice to a loving and respectful partner. There is no limit how high and rewarding, the positive fish swimming upstream, can lead a Virgo and his partner in life. Turning into a psychic Pisces facing the world, it would be foolish to lie to an advanced soul born in September. Less discriminating souls are very compassionate to the needs of others, and once more they could easily be manipulated for less than a glamorous ending. Facing the world as a soft Pisces, your advanced or less advanced male or female friend born in September could lend himself into one of these endeavors: computer science, television, cinematography, photography, writing, law, medicine, clinical medicine, psychiatry, or a very rewarding position in psychic work.

Virgo, House Number 8

Let's see what is going on in House Number 8 for those born in September. Look at House Number 8 in the Section Housing System for keywords. In the area of life and death, legacy, metaphysics, sex and corporate money, your male or female Virgo friend becomes a competitive Aries. Aries rules the head and many souls born in September are prone to suffer heavy migraine headaches. Others are prone to violent accidents on the head that could permanently damage the cerebral working of the physical body. Thus, Virgo is strongly advised not to take any chances, especially when alcohol or chemicals have been consumed. This House rules insurance, and many Virgos will receive financial settlements or indirect help from others' similar judicial endeavors. Aries is a leader and those born in September have great potential to build a long lasting financial security once they realize their true values and gifts and initiate a business of their own. Aries wants to be number one in all his endeavors; including the affair of sex. This motivation comes from a subconscious financial and sexual inferiority complex. The 8th House deals with sex, and as Aries rules the head of the body, your male or female friend born in September needs both mental and physical stimulation in bed. Aries is competitive in nature and the young Virgo soul will turn into a wild conqueror scoring as many sexual partners as possible. The more advanced souls born in September have only the best to offer on both the physical and spiritual sides of themselves. The 8th House involves corporate money and business resources; thus, Virgo has been given the potential to lead in all the elements involving the affairs of this particular House.

Virgo, House Number 9

How does your Virgo friend feels or behave in House Number 9? Let us see by looking at House Number 9 in the Section Housing System and read the keywords and get more information. This is the area of religion, traveling, learning, teaching, publishing and relationships with foreigners. In this area your male or female Virgo friend becomes a solid Taurus. Taurus is ruled by Venus, or in Greek mythology "The Goddess of Love." Because Taurus rules money, any effort put on education or dealing with foreigners will bring financial rewards to Virgo. The soul must find himself first then use the creative forces of Venus to further a form of light and teach the world. In this Taurus rational House, many young Virgo souls will become professional students and will not be allowed to perceive anything else that is not scientifically proven. This earthy attitude slows down cosmic consciousness and transforms the soul into a preacher of dogmas or a mental snob. The advanced Virgo soul knows better and will not miss the spirit for the printed word. In this, he or she is not afraid to be educated outside of what books coach one into. Once the independent self and the celestial truth is reached, those born in September are given the opportunity to become leaders in the House of teaching and publishing. Many Virgo souls will reach the masses and must pass on the knowledge without spiritual pride. Virgo is extremely curious and critical by nature and this Mercury ruled sign does regenerate in learning and teaching others. Taurus rules money and the banking industry, thus, many successful Virgo souls not only will travel the world around but will also have bank accounts outside of their country of birth. Thus, many famous Virgos have reached the best of their intellectual and spiritual expression and operate also outside of their country of birth and deal very well with foreigners and publishing. This Taurus money House brings them enormous financial rewards. This House rules the Indians, animals, traveling, and teaching the masses at large.

Virgo, House Number 10

Let us now get in to House Number 10. This is the area of career, public standing, and accomplishments. In this area your male or female Virgo friend becomes a dual Gemini. So now let's look at House Number 10 in the Section Housing System and read the keywords and get more information. Remember you can also refer to the Sun Sign Characteristics and read all about this Sun Sign. Mercury or "The Messenger of the Gods" in Greek mythology rules Gemini. Thus, your male or female Virgo friend has been given the opportunity to deal with many careers or has become a leader in the field of communication.

Mercury means also work via the telephone, radio, sales, writing, photography, and transportation. Additionally, Virgo is attracted to journalism, and many turn themselves into transcribers, editors, or attorneys. Chances are that your local emergency service driver or the boss of a large and successful telecommunications company was born in September. In the medical aspect of astrology, Virgo rules the digestive track, and your Virgo friend might be prone to indigestion, food poisoning or head injury. However, souls born in September are always aware of their commitment to further health and purity in the world, and will do all they can to fulfill that purpose. Your male or female friend born in September has a tendency to impose the rigid rules of the "Virgin Mary," thus, making your life miserable. Gemini rules the mind, and in the 10th House of career all will recognize the potential and intellectual value of Virgo.

Virgo, House Number 11

How does your male or female friend born in September feel about friends? So now let's look at House Number 11 in the Section Housing System and read the keywords and get more information. Remember you can also refer to the Sun Sign Characteristics and read all about this Sun Sign. This is the area of wishes, friends, and group organizations. In this area Virgo becomes a soft Cancer. The Moon rules this House and the sign of Cancer. Knowing that Cancer rules food, security, and real estate, your male or female friend born in September will surely attract caring friends. Sometimes Virgo involves a close friend or a family member in a business venture. Cancer is the sign of food, thus, your Virgo friend will treat you like a family member and will cook for you. We know too that Cancer loves to cook, thus, both parties will benefit from each other's caring and feeding attitude. This House rules also wishes, and as a Cancer, your Virgo friend has a serious desire to own a House and will take care of his friends and family at all times. Cancer is an emotional sign, thus, your male or female Virgo acquaintance friend will be reluctant to let go of close friends, and when they lose one they feel really sad. Like an emotional Cancer, Virgo can become easily hurt or too possessive with those they do care for. Turning into a Cancer on the friends and wishes House, Virgo will also spend money on many items for their home, friends and family. Virgo also loves antiques and they know the value of all they wish to acquire. It is part of their Cancerian attribute to treat you super well, just to reward you for being such a good friend. In this wishes House, Virgo becomes a Cancer, and this sign is a water sign, thus, living close to the water is part of a Cancer craving. Cancer rules beautiful classy restaurants and spas; thus, a good massage after a copious candlelight diner is always a wish for your Virgo friend. Cancer rules real estate, and part of your Virgo friend's wish is to own such a property so that he or she can feed the world physically and spiritually. Friends born in May, January and July will be attracted to Virgo, and many will revolve around them. Always remember to treat your Virgo friend right, as he or she becomes an oversensitive Cancer. Their deep feelings and true care will be offered unselfishly to you.

Virgo, House Number 12

Let's now investigate what going on in the subconscious area of your male or female friend born in September. Look at House Number 12 in the Section Housing System and read the keywords to get more information. Remember you can also refer to the Sun Sign Characteristics and read all about this Sun Sign. This is the area of fear, the subconscious, the imagination, and deception, of which traditionally Pisces rules. In this area Virgo becomes a powerful Leo. Virgo is a Mercurial sign and loves to talk, but the subconscious is a private area. Thus, it is important for those born in September to keep secrets, especially when friends and family are concerned. Souls born in September will also talk to themselves a lot. Virgo rules health, and many of the subconscious fears go in that direction. Being so concerned with health by nature and worrying about it could haunt the soul for life. Reacting as a Leo, the sign of youth and life, a subconscious fear of death or decay could be ever present. Leo also rules the 5th House of love, and in the 12th House of secret affairs your male or female friend born in September could be deceiving themselves with love. It is important for them to control the fear of not being good enough or the fear of not finding real love. They must understand that beauty is not only physical but also spiritual. Unlike their physical body, their loving, beautiful spiritual nature will never fade away. As Leo rules fame, many September souls could gain recognition by writing about love, children or health. The downfall is usually coming from a strong hidden spiritual pride where the young Virgo soul thinks he knows better than others. The advanced Virgo has learned humility and possesses the golden key of true knowledge.

Astropsychology Profile
Libra

Let's now read all about those born in October. Venus, ruler of Libra gives your friends born in October the opportunity to establish love, balance, and harmony in all areas of their life. Libra is an air sign and needs mental stimulation and must avoid any situation that could jeopardize their sensitive balance.

Libra, House Number 1

The soul's purpose of your friends born in October is to aim for equilibrium and establish a sense of balance in all areas of life. Sensitive and caring, the advanced Libra will teach the world the highest laws to improve peace and love in the world. Many souls born in October also write or speak about those laws. Look at House Number 1 in the Section Housing System and read the keywords and get more information. The negative aspect of this sign is to become a professional student of a specific chosen religious doctrine and impose the rigorous dogmatic rules unto others. Those young souls born in October are simply looking for themselves and may become totally unbalanced, even fanatic to anything else than the teaching of their own particular choice of religion. Born to promote the law of both the physical and spiritual manifestation, the advanced Libra soul's teachings will improve anyone's spiritual life. Many souls born in October work for the well-being of humanity and do also well with paperwork. Their keen mind is well suited for exploration and investigations and could lead the young soul to study religion; psychology or the legal profession. The advanced Libra soul is fast to realize the real power of Astropsychology and establishes the true correlation between the physical mind and the spiritual mind. In the process, a true understanding of the laws is established between the spiritual and physical worlds, and a firm balance of the mind, to bring about a clarification of a true human behavioral nature. Your male or female friend born in October is an intellectual, and translation of any laws will appeal to them. The young soul will fall victim of religious poisoning and may travel the world imposing his archaic views to the world. On the medical aspect of Astropsychology Libra rules the kidneys. The kidneys cleansing principle provides a perfect balance in health. Libra can be as judgmental as the very teaching they try so hard to avoid. A well-balanced Libra will see to it and will keep his religious convictions private and won't be afraid to investigate a new set of laws.

Libra, House Number 2

How does your male or female friend born in October behave in the money area? Look at House Number 2 in the Section Housing System and read the keywords and get more information. Libra's 2nd House of money is located in the powerful sign of Scorpio. This sign rules other people's money, insurances, legacy, investment, the medical world and metaphysics to name a few. Many people born in October will attract partners and must deal with contracts. You will find Libra almost anywhere where a strong sense of justice, investigation, organization of others' resources, investment, research and health is concerned. Libra does work for the church real estate, education, the food industry, hotels, etc. The ability they possess to investigate another's resources and make it grow is a serious gift. It is often used by organized business enterprises where a persons funds or property is manipulated for the abusive institutions financial and selfish end. Libra operates well in a quiet office, especially if research, corporate money, health or private communication is requested. The swift thinking they were born with is the perfect gift needed to explore both sides of a question and establish the just middle. Because Libra rules the law and contracts, your male or female friends born in October may find themselves involved with large religious institutions, corporations and governmental rules. They are adept at finding solutions to gather the financial support of others, thus, furthering the sense of balance and harmony they so desperately need for themselves. On a negative aspect, the wrong or ill use of another's resources becomes a doomed endeavor for Libra, and they usually end up in court. On a very negative note, by using and or abusing others, the soul ends up in jail or meets with an early death. Many of my students who do master the Universal Laws are using Astropsychology positively, and as a means for living. Note: Libra author John Gray, **Men are from Mars, Women from Venus**, consulted with me and purchased my Astropsychology album course at the San Francisco Whole Expo conference.

Libra, House Number 3

In their 3rd House your friends born in October become a philosophical Sagittarius. So now let's look at House Number 3 in the Section Housing System and read the keywords to gather more information. The opportunity is given to your male or female Libra friend to investigate all man made philosophies in any given country. Sagittarius rules also the Indian world, and pets. On a negative note, the young Libra soul could involve himself in heavy gambling. The direct approach of the centaur or Sagittarius will be felt through their speech. Remember that a young Libra soul sees and reacts only to what his religion has taught him as the supreme law. In their eyes, anything else is not the truth they are looking for. Sadly enough for them, the very chance to improve their cosmic consciousness is alienated with this rigid type of intellectual attitude. The advanced ones keep a strong hold on their belief system, are very curious by nature and avoid criticizing others religious or spiritual values openly. The advanced Libra soul regenerates with the study of metaphysics, investments, science, health, Astropsychology and anything demanding spiritual gymnastics. Thus, your male or female friend born in October inherited a deep philosophical mind and needs to explore the world to find the truth. Those born in October must realize the incredible spiritual potential offered to them but must not miss the spirit looking at the printed religious words. Instead, through critical thinking and education they can further their own cosmic consciousness and reach the celestial truth through the zodiac. The mind of a Libra is well suited to do any spiritual work. The regeneration principle takes place through learning, teaching, traveling, investigating, health and mastering the laws of the Universal Mind through Astropsychology. The thought process becomes very powerful allowing them to find answers to teach solutions to almost anything. Once the dogmatic thinking process is eliminated and fear is removed, Libra can find peace of mind and happiness in every area of his life.

Libra, House Number 4

So now let's look in House Number 4 for those born in October. In the home area, your male or female Libra friend becomes an organized and business oriented Capricorn. Look at House Number 4 in the Section Housing System and read the keywords for more information. This is the sign of structure and represents Libra's desire to control and manage the domestic scene accordingly. The goat lives high in the mountain and Libra needs to live in an elevated area. Capricorn needs a position of respect and many will choose to own a house in one of the most distinguished areas of the city. Many souls born in October regenerate by listening to classical music, handling plants and by doing gardening work. Capricorn's organizational strength is at home and may influence your friend born in October to run a business from home. Your Libra friend needs to have a very organized environment where he or she can build, and even structure a great career. Meantime, if you are dealing with a young soul, your Libra friend is much too busy dreaming or is doing the wrong things to organize his home life. Venus rules Libra and laziness is also part of the weakest aspect of this sign's desire for an easy life. Usually Libra is raised in a firm and structured environment where strict or religious rules are usually enforced at an early age. Being naturally susceptible to any teaching of the laws, the subconscious

I Know All About You

desire to re-establish those rules around them is also quite strong. Many Libra souls can be overwhelming at home and will suffer tremendously if one of their children refuses to obey or reject these laws. These early religious teachings usually generate a variety of hang-ups and can seriously alter the soul's perception of sex as a corrupt thing to do. However, with discrimination, the Libra soul frees himself from the puritanical mental attitude and does find balance and harmony with his children.

Libra, House Number 5

Let's move on to the 5th House of love and romance and see what or how your Libra male or female friend becomes when touched by love. Look at House Number 5 in the Section Housing System and read the keywords. Libra turns into an original Aquarius in this House. Thus, Libra will attract those born in June, February or April. It is important to remember that, regardless of the month of your birth, the attraction can also be coming from any sign of the zodiac. Chances are that the attraction will be coming directly from the location of the hidden Dragon in those signs. Thus, as Aquarius rules Astropsychology, your male or female friend born in October is now given the opportunity to explore and speculate the working of the Universal Mind and free the spirit from the rigid and limited religious doctrines. They are original in matters of love and demand to travel the world with the partner. Libra will not get involved with anyone just for the sake of having a relationship. Beauty and health are important to them but they need more from you, they also need mental stimulation. This is the House of speculation and research, thus many Libras will travel the world to research the truth. On a more practical level as Aquarius energy rules Hi Tech, the Water Bearer may turn your male or female friend into a pilot, airhostess, a computer wiz, a television host, a UFO researcher or an astrologer. Aquarius rules group endeavors where the truth is investigated and exposed. A good friend of mine (Libra) Bob Brown is the President of International UFO Congress, Inc; incidentally, Bob is also an airline pilot. You may contact him at 303-543-9443 if you are into UFO research. In that respect not many people will match their extraordinary standards for the truth and the Universal Aquarius love they are able to offer to the world. The advanced soul takes on the challenges imposed by this House and ultimately gains remarkable rewards. The motivation is produced by a true love for humanity and its origin.

Libra, House Number 6

In the 6th House of work, health, and service, souls born in October become the vulnerable Pisces. Look at House Number 6 in the Section Housing System for the keywords. This zodiac sign was chosen subconsciously by Christianity and rules all religions. Neptune, "Lord of the Seas," can be extremely deceptive and misleading. Souls falling in his quicksand may never return to sanity. Because this is the House of health, it is important to mention that all of those born in October were born with a negative reaction to chemicals, drugs, alcohol, doctor prescriptions etc., especially if the span of attention is short and prone to fall asleep quickly. In that respect many young Libra souls will fall prey for organized religions and will offer their services to the world for free. A strong guilt feeling is present and must be recognized to avoid being used and abused by any institution. The advanced ones will involve or deal with chemicals or oil in their working life while others are truly gifted actors, musicians, painters, dancers and remarkable doctors of the mind. You will often find a Libra working as a nurse or as a psychic. However, Pisces is underhanded and the mastering of the rigid rules of the Universal Mind can bring about an incredible perception of the human nature. Many of my students of Astropsychology were born in October and do well with any group organization, traveling, and teaching the world. Others would rather work from home and do become writers and publishers. Thus, your male or female friend born in October is very committed to others and could easily be manipulated at work, all of this because they are humanitarian at heart. The strong Libra's sense of harmony combined with the illusive, unselfish Pisces service House could make them prone to abuses. Pisces is altruistic in nature and a true Libra will exhibit a strong friendship attitude with co-workers. A well-balanced and peaceful environment at work is a must for those born in October. Thus, Pisces must swim upstream towards creativity and practicability in all they do to service the world. In extreme cases, the strong pull of the negative fish can lead the soul towards a fanatical pious life, and produce a nun or a priest. Libra means servicing the world with the laws while Pisces is the opportunity to reach for the clear water of unpolluted truth. Pisces' higher purpose will allow many souls born in October to offer their true spiritual gift to the world.

Libra, House Number 7

So now let's look in the House of marriage and how those born in October deal with their partners. In the 7th House of relationships, your male or female Libra friend becomes a very competitive Aries. Look at House Number 7 in the

Section Housing System for the keywords. Because Aries is an aggressive sign, many Libras will demand and attract strong business partners. Aries is a fire sign and has not much patience with dreamers; thus, they are motivated by action and have little tolerance for sensitive dreamers. Because of the impatient nature of Aries they could also slow down success by being over demanding or too direct in business. Because of the self centered attitude and impetuosity of this Mars ruled sign, your Libra friend can become an easy pray to a soft-spoken manipulator by boosting the Aries ego. Mars, the ruler of Aries rules action, fire, danger, engineering, and machinery; thus, Libra will attract competitive partners. Aries rules the 1st House of the "self" and many young souls born in October must learn and practice diplomacy if they are to keep a smooth relationship. Those acquaintances are usually met on the social scene and introduced by another competitive friend. Your advanced male or female friend born in October is willing to sacrifice himself to save or improve any relationship. However, the desire to keep harmony should not interfere when the need to stand strong is needed. The competitive Aries nature will make them feel confident in dealing with the world and others. The advanced Libra soul is a master of diplomacy and has no problem offering true love, respect and sacrifice to a loving and respectful partner. There is no limit how high and rewarding, the Aries spirit, can lead a Libra and his chosen partner in life. Less advanced souls are constantly battling with life and pay the price with their egotistical nature and with loneliness. Facing the world as a well-balanced person, your male or female friend born in October was born with all the tools to succeed in any endeavor. Computers, investments, construction, science, television, cinematography, photography, writing, and the legal system all appeal to them.

Libra, House Number 8

Let's see what going on in House Number 8 for those born in October. Look at House Number 8 in the Section Housing System for keywords. In the area of life and death, legacy, metaphysics, sex and corporate money, your male or female Libra friend becomes a solid Taurus. Taurus rules the esophagus and all the neck glands, and under stress many souls born in October are prone to induce stress in these areas. Others are prone to indulge themselves with too much of the good things in life that could permanently damage the good workings of the heart. Thus, Libra is strongly advised to get active and exercise regularly. This House rules investments and insurance and many Libras will receive financial settlements or reap the benefits of their investments. Taurus is the money sign and rules also Switzerland where much of the world's financial assets are secured. This sign is patient and practical; thus, those born in October have a great potential to build a long lasting financial security. Libra needs partners while Taurus is reluctant to share anything with anyone. However, the advanced Libra realizes the importance of a partner's resources and the financial potential involved. They are willing to share once a solid, practical well-balanced contract has been established from all parties involved. This House also rules affairs of sex, and Taurus is a very sensual sign. On a negative note, the young Libra soul will use his financial position to financially control the partner for sexual gratification. This motivation comes from Taurus' subconscious desire for financial and sexual control over those he deeply cares for. Because Taurus is a wealthy sign, your male or female friend born in October needs to feel only the best in the foods they eat, and in the environment in which they live, as that will produce mental and physical stimulation in bed. Taurus is solid and needs a long and lasting love, and passionate sex. To them, financial security means the power to afford the best of what life has to offer, including sex. The more advanced souls born in October have only the best to offer on both the physical and spiritual side of themselves. The 8th House involves corporate money and business resources, thus, Libra has been given the potential to build and gain from all the elements involving the affairs of this particular House.

Libra, House Number 9

How does your Libra friend feel or behave in the area of religion, traveling, learning, teaching, publishing, and relationships with foreigners? In this House your male or female Libra friend becomes a witty Gemini. Mercury, "The Messenger of the Gods" rules Gemini in Greek mythology. Because Gemini rules sales and communications of all sorts, dealing with foreigners will bring opportunities and financial rewards to Libra. Gemini rules duality, thus, chances are that your male or female friend born in October will deal with more than one foreigner at time. This House involves also teaching and traveling, thus, many Libras do a lot of traveling, teaching others, and establishing contracts wherever their business mind takes them. In the 9th House, the soul must establish himself in a foreign environment by using the creative forces of Mercury. Venus, the ruler of Libra loves beauty, money and enjoys the best that life has to offer. Your male or female friend born in October will initiate or find party partners to bring about the opportunity they are looking for to further their business ideas to others. In this House your Libra friend becomes a dual Gemini and the superb adaptation of this sign will attract those who have similar wishes or interests. Gemini rules also newsletters, communication, radio, errands, flyers, and advertisements; in the House of higher learning, many Libras will find happiness teaching others the art of promotional sales. Like Gemini, Libra is an air sign and does regenerate in learning and teaching others. Thus, many Libras have reached the best of their intellectual and spiritual expression and operate also outside of their country of birth and deal very well with foreigners and publishing. The 9th House also rules the Indians, animals, traveling and teaching the masses at large.

Libra, House Number 10

Let's now get into House Number 10. This is the area of career, public standing and accomplishments. In this area your male or female Libra friend becomes a caring Cancer. So now let's look at House Number 10 in the Section Housing System and read the keywords to get more information. Remember you can also refer to the Sun Sign Characteristics and read all about this Sun Sign. The Moon rules Cancer, thus, your male or female Libra friend has been given the opportunity to feed, to care for and protect others in a chosen career. Many Libra's involve themselves successfully in real estate, hotels, the food industry, and some of them use their home as a meeting place for business. Cancer controls this House and the moon rules this sign. Thus, the awareness and use of the Moon's fluctuations is an important part of planning and a sure chance for success. Chances are that your local store manager or restaurant owner was born in October or inherited a strong hidden Dragon in Cancer. In the medical aspect of astrology, Libra rules the kidneys and your friend born in October might be prone to backache or insomnia. Your male or female Libra friend can also be found in the construction field, building homes, selling furniture even working for Uncle Sam or a very large corporation; all the while working hard to bring about emotional, and physical security to the people they serve so perfectly. Cancer rules silver, and the advanced Libra businessman work in retrieving or improving this product from the earth.

Libra, House Number 11

How does your male or female friend born in October feel or behave with friends? This is the area of wishes, friends and group organization. In this area Libra becomes a shining Leo. So now let's look at House Number 11 in the Section Housing System and read the keywords to get more information. Remember you can also refer to the Sun Sign Characteristics and read all about the sign of Leo. The Sun rules this House and knowing that Leo rules love, romance, children, the stage, the arts, your male or female friend born in October will surely attract interesting friends. Sometimes Libra's involve close friends in business ventures as long as the partner understands and realizes that Libra will need a total commitment from them. Leo is the sign of party and love; thus, your Libra friend may be a channel for love to others. Libra can also end up marrying a long-standing friend introduced years earlier by another friend. Leo rules France and Italy, thus your male or female friend born in October will have friends from these countries. We also know that Leo loves to entertain and many enjoy fame, thus, many of Libra's friends will be light promoters or well known to the rest of the world. This House rules also wishes, and turning into a loyal Leo, your Libra friend may demand attention and will do all he can to prove to you that you have a very special friend. Leo is a fire sign, thus, your male or female Libra friend will be promoting close friends that are involved in the arts or those willing to further love and the light. This House is ruled by the Sun and on a negative note, your Libra friend can become easily egocentric or too possessive with those they do care for. Like a Lion your Libra friend needs to be in charge, and will take pride of doing the best he or she can do for their friends. No one else can do better than the King to turn Libra's close friends into resentful souls. The strong inner desire to do better than any of their friends, moves your Libra friend to spend quite a lot of money to assure superiority over them. However, a legitimate desire to help all and any "friend" is also a pure part of their motivation.

Libra, House Number 12

Let's now investigate what is going on in the subconscious area of your male or female friend born in October. This is the area of fear, imagination, the subconscious and deception traditionally ruled by Pisces. In this House your male or female friend born in October becomes a critical Virgo. Look at House Number 12 in the Section Housing System and read some of the keywords to get more information. Remember you can also refer to the Sun Sign Characteristics and read all about the Sun Sign of Virgo. Virgo is a Mercurial sign and loves to talk, but the subconscious is a private area. Thus, it is important for those born in October to keep secrets, especially when friends and family are concerned. Souls born in October will also talk a lot to themselves too. Virgo rules health and purity, thus, much of their subconscious fears may go in that direction. Being so concerned with health and a perfectionist at heart, your Libra friend may feel concerned and criticize the bad habits of others. Reacting as Virgo, the sign of perfection and service to the world, your Libra friend may carry a subconscious fear of not doing enough work. Virgo also rules the 6th House of work and in the 12th House of secret affairs your male or female friend born in October could be doing a lot of work at night and behind the scenes. It is important for them to control the fear of not being active enough or the fear of not finding the real truth around them. A subconscious desire for chastity and purity may also lead to a myriad of subconscious fears of disease. Your Libra friend must understand that nothing is perfect in this dense physical world and beauty is not only physical but also spiritual. Virgo rules work and health, and many Libra souls are concerned with ones health and service to the world. In the process of providing only the best to others, the Virginal puritanical attitude of Virgo can become overbearing in the search of perfection. The advanced Libra soul has reached peace and harmony in both the physical and spiritual worlds, and many possess the golden key of true knowledge.

Astropsychology Profile Scorpio

Let's now explore souls born in November. Pluto is the ruler of this intense water sign and will give your friends born in November beautiful magnetic eyes and an incredible will power. Scorpio must learn to control and channel Pluto's power constructively. Pluto rules also life and death, drama, the police force, the mafia, the medical field, witchcraft, the rebirthing process, etc. The opportunity to regenerate in investigation, creation and high science is offered to the soul.

Scorpio, House Number 1

The soul's purpose of your friends born in November is to aim for the Eagle or the Phoenix in himself and get to the bottom or the top of any and all of his earthy experiences. Scorpio is constantly looking for the answers of what it means to be human. Intense, passionate, magnetic and strong willed, it takes a powerful soul to deal with a superior Scorpio. Your friend born in November will always teach something to whoever is daring to fly with him. So now let's look at House Number 1 in the Section Housing System and read the keywords to gather more information. The negative aspect of this sign is to use the nasty and poisonous dart under the form of sarcasm and impose an overbearing will unto others. The young Scorpio soul is also called "The Lizard" and will use all means to take revenge and destroy its enemy. Young souls born in November can be ruthless and dangerous to themselves and society. Your male or female friend born in November is a very intense person and may not necessarily spare your feelings if you ask him or her a direct question. In extreme cases, the destructive emotional side of this sign can lead the soul into jail and produce a dangerous criminal. Born to control passion in a life full of drama, the advanced Scorpio soul is a very special gift and will improve anyone's life. Your male or female friend born in November must work for a greater purpose. Their keen mind is well suited for explorations and investigations. Many Scorpios are found in the medical profession, engineering, the police force, and any endeavor demanding supreme physical, intellectual, artistic or spiritual quality. A well-balanced Scorpio will see his poisoned stinger and will remove it before using it against himself or the world around him. Read *The Power of the Dragon* and understand "The Death Wish Generation," or the children killing children in our colleges and universities. These souls were born with Pluto, the ruler of Scorpio in his/her own sign (Scorpio), and produced this generation of killers.

Scorpio, House Number 2

So now let's look at the self-esteem and the money area for those born in November. Look at House Number 2 in the Section Housing System and read the keywords to get more awareness on the affairs of this House. Scorpio's 2nd House of money is located in the Sign of Sagittarius. This fire sign rules the law, foreign land, Spain, Portugal, Australia, education, traveling, publishing and the codification of thoughts. You will always find a November soul almost anywhere where learning, teaching, dedication, organization, research and health is concerned. Because Sagittarius rules foreign lands and publishing worldwide, many Scorpio's establish financial security. This House also deals with self-esteem, thus, traveling and operating overseas is always healing and progressive for Scorpio. On the negative aspect, your male or female friend born in November may fall for the worse side of Sagittarius and become a compulsive gambler. The blind faith produced by Jupiter combined with the Scorpio intensity could prove to be disastrous for a young soul born in November. Because Sagittarius rules also the law and Scorpio, corporate money, your male or female friends born in November could be involved with large corporations or enforcing Uncle Sam's rules. Jupiter rules the sign of Sagittarius and this planet is called in Greek mythology "The Lord of Expansion," thus, your Scorpio friend was born with the real potential to become very wealthy. This planet also rules publishing and many artistic oriented Scorpios were given the potential to do well in these areas. Other lucky souls born in November inherit from legacy and legal actions. Scorpio is adept at finding solutions and usually gathers the financial support of others. On a negative aspect, wrong financial endeavors are doomed when all the negative parties involved end up in court or in jail. Many Scorpios do very well in the arts, writing, and teaching.

Scorpio, House Number 3

The 3rd House rules the thinking process. In this House your friend born in November becomes a shrewd Capricorn. Investigate House Number 3 in the Section Housing System and read the keywords to gather more information. The opportunity to plan and gain recognition through an academic pursuit is a strong possibility for your male or female Scorpio. Capricorn rules large organizations, the government, structure, engineering, architecture and control over the working class. Many powerful political figures were born in November such as French President General De Gaulle, and Robert F. Kennedy. Combined with the power of Pluto (ruler of Scorpio), a young soul born in November can be the best mental manipulator around. The mind of the advanced Scorpio or "The Eagle" is never resting. The desire to penetrate the depth of a situation and find the right answer is extreme. So much mental command geared towards accomplishment gives Scorpio the power to accomplish practically anything under the Sun. The give away of a strong Scorpio in a chart is the intense gaze or beautiful green or blue magnetic eyes. On a negative note, the crude sarcasm will be felt through their speech. Remember that the Scorpio mind is incredibly astute and unless ready for the harsh truth, don't ask. Sadly enough for the young November soul, the very chance to launch a business or establish a relationship can be killed before it even starts. The advanced Scorpio knows your strengths as well as your weakness too well. As a rule your friends born in November will always regenerate with metaphysics, investments, science, health, astrology and anything demanding incredible mental concentration. Thus, your male or female Scorpio friend inherited a powerful practical mind and can easily probe your thoughts, motivations and feelings almost immediately. As always, wherever Scorpio is to be found in your chart one must avoid using the poisonous stinger of the Scorpion against others and especially against himself. Those born in November do realize the incredible mental potential they inherited and must destroy the stinger of the Scorpion. Through metaphysics Scorpio can further a unique cosmic consciousness and fly like an Eagle above it all. The mind is well suited to do absolutely anything and the regeneration principle takes place when investigating both physical and spiritual matters. On the negative side, the young Scorpio's mind will fall for the mental snobbism of Capricorn. He then becomes a super but trapped rational scientist. The mathematical aptitude and attention to detail makes it hard for the Eagle to fly pass the limits of the physical manifestation.

Scorpio, House Number 4

So now let's look in House Number 4 for those born in November. Look at House Number 4 in the Section Housing

System and read the keywords for more information. In the home area, your male or female Scorpio friend becomes a weird Aquarius. This original sign rules the future of mankind, the New Age and unique method of divination. The sign of Aquarius rules independence, computers and originality. In that respect many Scorpios may chose to live alone or use their home base as a place for private mental investigation. The House of a Scorpio is always special and anyone can feel the incredible amount of energy concentrated inside of the walls. They can also reside in a big city, but their home will always look like a portion of their intense emotional and private nature. Many regenerate with metaphysics, investigation, research, science and studying all the secrets of life. Scorpio means intensity, penetration, and intuition while Aquarius means Universal matters, electronics, the future and invention. So your friend born in November needs privacy in order to do the research he is aiming for. Aquarius rules also friends, thus, your Scorpio friend needs a variety of friends that could leave his house in a total mess after a night of gambling or drinking. Aquarius rules freedom oriented groups and videotaping while Scorpio rules sex; thus, the desire to explore original sex is always present. The young male or female Scorpio soul may use the negative side of his sexual nature through the use of electronics and travel the world via the Internet. Your male or female friend born in November may also find group sex stimulating as represented by the freedom-oriented sign of Aquarius. The advanced Eagle soul will make a more progressive use of the home base to promote cosmic consciousness or produce incredible results via electronics to the rest of the world.

Scorpio, House Number 5

Let's move on to the 5th House of love and romance, and

see what your Scorpio male or female friend becomes when he or she is touched by love. Look at House Number 5 in the Section Housing System and read the keywords. The very powerful Scorpio turns into a melodramatic, super emotional and over sensitive Pisces in this House. Thus, souls born in November will attract a Taurus, a Pisces or a Cancer. They could as always attract any sign of the zodiac that has something spiritual or artistic to offer. Like all water signs they do strive for sincerity, emotional fulfillment and security; this is usually found with another water sign. Scorpio is a water sign but could also be attracted to a fiery Leo or Sagittarius because of a hidden water Dragon in their partner's chart. Your male or female friend born in November is extremely emotional and is prone to let his deep emotions take over the practical mind. Super emotional in matters of love, Scorpio will not get involved with anyone just for the sake of having a relationship. Beauty and wealth are important to them but they do strive for passion and emotions in a close relationship. The Pisces power will make them overly sensitive but extremely caring. They are looking at you emotionally and will expect the same in return. Sadly enough, however, your male or female friend born in November may attract a karmic relationship and swim downstream towards self-destruction alcoholism and ultimately end up in jail. Scorpio rules power sex, respect, and ultimate accomplishments. Many young November souls never had a chance to let the world enjoy the true gift they do possess because of the over emotional and destructive fish in them. They must learn to apply the super will they possess and let go of the wrong people and destructive emotions. They need to know that their chosen partner is deserving, faithful, and giving true love instead of begging for it. Why waste time with someone who cannot take care of himself or is too weak to fly with the Eagle? They are capable of incredible sacrifices and will undoubtedly give their precious life away to those they love. Only a November soul is able to offer so much love, so much intensity and so much self-sacrifice. This is also the House of creativity and denotes the incredible artistic creativity and talent of Pisces.

Scorpio, House Number 6

In the 6th House of work, health, and service, souls born in November become competitive Aries. Look at House Number 6 in the Section Housing System for the keywords. This zodiac sign is ruled by Mars (The Lord of War) and this planet rules action, speed, danger and war. Thus, your male or female Scorpio friend is extremely competitive and may find it difficult to work with others. The young Scorpio soul must learn to control his temper and avoid fighting with others in the work environment. The powerful Martian spirit can be channeled productively and gives Scorpio the power to fight for the good of all. Under the power of Mars in the 6th House, your male or female friend born in November becomes fearless when facing death. Many Scorpio works for the police force, or where a gut is needed. Scorpio rules total power and the young soul may fall for a life of crime, sex, and passion in nightlife where danger, death and passion reign. The advanced Eagle will use and control the Martian energy intelligently and accomplish miracles during the course of their life. Because Scorpio rules investigation, night, health, life and death, your Scorpio friend will aim in that direction in their chosen career. This sign is very intense and extremely emotional in nature and a true Scorpio will exhibit a strong leadership attitude with co-workers. A well-balanced and peaceful environment at work is a must for those born in November. Under stress Scorpio may develop headaches and sinus problems. Many of them end up with many scars on their head or face. Pluto (the ruler of Scorpio) rules also metaphysics, the medical field, insurance, corporate money, and investigation. Your male or female friend born in November must feel that he or she is part of an important purpose that will promote mankind.

Scorpio, House Number 7

So now let's look in the House of marriage and see how those born in November deal with the world. In the 7th House of relationships, your male or female Scorpio friend becomes a solid and stubborn Taurus. Look at House Number 7 in the Section Housing System for the keywords. Venus, "The Goddess of Love" rules the arts in this House, thus, Scorpio will attract beautiful and artistic partners. Because Taurus rules money and security, many Scorpios will also attract wealthy, strong and controlling partners. On a negative note, your male or female friend born in November could become an unyielding and possessive Taurus with his partner; thereby, becoming the legendary jealous, possessive, and stubborn Taurus who will not let go of a dying relationship. Taurus is a security-oriented sign and the keywords for Taurus are "I have and I possess". Pluto (the ruler of Scorpio), rules power and sex, and combined with Scorpio's dramatic touch, furnishes a constant flux; a sexual urge of energy, which revitalizes the relationship. The young Scorpio soul must realize that no one possesses or ultimately controls anyone else, and when they realize this, they realize that letting go of a decaying relationship is also an act of love. Your male or female friend faces the world as a "bull" and on the medical aspect of Astropsychology; Taurus rules the throat, music and singing. Thus, you will find many November souls charming you with their warm voices and incredible musical talent. Never forget that you are dealing with a soft, artistic, romantic soul in public. However, those horns could prove to be extremely dangerous as represented by one of the most dangerous and unpredictable animals in the bush; that is the African buffalo. Learning to let go of a partner is indeed the most difficult lesson a November soul must learn. Once this is done, usually through drama, the Eagle takes over and rewards Scorpio with a true loving and sensitive partner.

Scorpio, House Number 8

Let's see what going on in House Number 8 for those born in November. Look at House Number 8 in the Section Housing System for keywords. In the area of life and death, legacy, metaphysics, sex and corporate money, your male or female Scorpio becomes witty Gemini. Scorpio rules sex and Gemini duality, thus, the young soul born in November may explore sex with many partners. Gemini needs communication and the 8th House deals with sex. Thus, your male or female friend born in November needs plenty of variety and both mental and physical stimulation in bed. The advanced ones will get mental stimulation and will offer intellectual stimulation and variation to their partners. The sign of Gemini rules photography, books and all forms of communication. In some sexual way, souls born in November will involve themselves in that direction. The 8th House deals also with metaphysics, corporate money, affairs of the dead and legacy; thus, your Scorpio friend will read and educate himself on many of these topics. This is the House of death, thus, all souls born in November could develop and suffer respiratory problems if he or she is under constant stress. Others are prone to violent death or accidents on the head that could permanently damage the rest of the body. Thus, Scorpio is strongly advised not to let their powerful and destructive emotions take over especially when alcohol has been consumed. This House rules brothers and sisters and many Scorpios could lose a brother or a sister or end up taking care of a close family member or help them in a judicial endeavor. In this House, Scorpio becomes an intellectual Gemini and with it the great potential to become a speaker or write books on many spiritual or financial topics. A great friend of mine, David Oates was born in November and he is well knows all over the world for his incredible investigative reverse speech techniques. Scorpio means sex while Gemini variety; the young Scorpio soul will turn into a wild conqueror scoring and collecting pictures of as many sexual partners as possible. The more advanced souls born in November have only the best to offer of both the physical and spiritual sides of themselves.

Scorpio, House Number 9

How does your Scorpio friend feel or behave in House Number 9? Look at House Number 9 in the Section Housing System and read the keywords and get more information. This is the area of religion, traveling, learning, teaching, publishing and relationships with foreigners. In this area your male or female Scorpio friend becomes an emotional Cancer. The Moon and this sign rules food,

hotels, casinos and restaurants. Thus, you will find many souls born in November feeding the world and owning property in foreign lands. Because Cancer rules also real estate, your November friend will spend money and education in this direction. The 9th House deals also with publishing, traveling, education and dealing with foreigners. Doing so will bring financial rewards to your male or

I Know All About You 149

female friend born in November. The very successful Scorpio will spend much of his time away from home and will enjoy the best of the best of many glamorous hotels. In this Cancer emotional and traveling House, many Scorpio souls will develop very strong ties with foreigners and will become part of their family. In this Cancer caring House, the advanced Scorpio will work hard to feed, protect and provide a more secure world for the benefit of mankind. Many November souls take on long and far away journeys to fulfill their fate. Many of them are passionate and cry about their past, their family, the people they left behind and their hometown. Because the moon rules Cancer, it is important for them to understand and use the Moon's fluctuations in all aspects of this House. This sign is a water sign and many souls born in November do travel the world's oceans or spend quality time on a cruise. Once the celestial truths are reached, those born in November are given the opportunity to feed the world through metaphysical teaching and publishing. This Cancer caring House brings them enormous spiritual and financial rewards. This House also rules the Indians, animals, traveling and teaching the masses at large.

Scorpio, House Number 10

Let's now get in to House Number 10. This is the area of career, public standing and accomplishments. In this area your male or female Scorpio friend becomes a powerful Leo. So now lets look at House Number 10 in the Section Housing System and read the keywords and get more information. Remember you can also refer to the Sun Sign Characteristics and read all about Leo's sign. The Sun or "The Light Bringer" in Greek mythology rules Leo. Thus, your male or female Scorpio friend has been given the opportunity to reach fame and fortune or become a leader in the artistic field. Leo means also light, life and the stage, thus, Scorpio is also attracted to any profession where children are concerned. Many November souls turn themselves into beacons of fame such as Larry King, Charles Bronson, Richard Burton, Prince Charles and Ted Turner. Incidentally, ex French President Charles De Gaulle was also born in November, and in his 10th House of Career he was a Leo, and this sign rules France. Chances are that your local bar, restaurant owner, surgeon, artist or the boss of a large and successful business was born in November. In the medical aspect of astrology, Leo rules the heart, thus, your Scorpio friend might be prone to an early heart attack if too much stress comes from the career endeavor. You will also find November souls in your local school system or in your local hospital helping the children of the world to grow or get better. Your male or female friend born in November can also misuse an overbearing Leo will and impose a very bossy mind-set upon others. This egocentric attitude could make any Scorpio employees' life misery. On a more positive note, the advanced Scorpio soul will use the creative forces of the Sun constructively and provide a constant source of stimulation and success to others.

Scorpio, House Number 11

How does your male or female friend born in November feel about friends? Let's look at House Number 11 in the Section Housing System and read the keywords and get more information. This is the area of wishes, friends and group organization. In this section of life your Scorpio friend becomes a critical Virgo. Remember you can also refer to the Sun Sign characteristics and read all about this Sun Sign. The planet Mercury rules this House and the sign of Virgo. Knowing that Virgo rules health and organization, your male or female friend born in November will nurture a wish for servicing the world at large. In that respect, Scorpio does attract Pisces and Virgo friends. Your male or female friend born in November will never let you down and will do all he or she can to help you to establish yourself. However, they do expect you to take care of yourself once true, physical or spiritual help has been provided. Scorpio is quite critical of their close friends and a major mistake can be fatal to your friendship. Virgo is the sign of health, organization, plants and purification; thus, your Scorpio friend has a wish to bring about purity to the world through a vocational career. Virgo loves to clean and reorganize the body. Thus, a desire to use homeopathic or alternative medicine is always present. Virgo is not exactly an emotional sign, thus, your male or female November friend will be cutting and cold with close friends. Thus, do not let the infamous Scorpio dart get to you if you have a friend born in November and don't expect him or her to be too diplomatic with you. It is part of their Virgo critical attributes to make you aware of your weaknesses but if a Scorpio has picked you as a friend, you surely are someone special. Virgo rules beautiful clothes, health and spas, thus, a good massage after a hard day's work is always a wish for your Scorpio friend.

Scorpio, House Number 12

Let's now investigate what is going on in the subconscious area of your male or female friend born in November. Look at House Number 12 in the Section Housing System and read the keywords to get more information. This is the area of fear, imagination, the subconscious and deception traditionally ruled by Pisces. In this House Scorpio becomes a sensitive Libra. Remember you can also refer to the Sun Sign Characteristics and read all about this Sun Sign. Libra is a Venusian sign and needs balance, harmony, and of course a committed partner to love. Thus, it is important for those born in November to be in a well-balanced and harmonious relationship. This House rules secret affairs and as a rule, Scorpio will only share emotional information only to those very close to him, especially when friends and family are concerned. Because Libra is a wealthy and gracious sign, your November friend has a subconscious desire for marrying well. Subconsciously souls born in November demand total commitment and honesty from their partners. On a negative note, the young Scorpio soul will plot or plan and secretively spy on the partner's activity. Libra rules marriage, beauty, balance and harmony and much of the subconscious fears may be coming from a lack of trust. Your male or female friend born in November is very concerned with keeping justice and harmony at all time, however, this is rarely possible and could haunt the soul for life. Reacting as Libra, the sign of love, a subconscious fear of loneliness or emotional decay could be present. Libra also rules the 7th House of marriage and in the 12th House of secret affairs your male or female friend born in November could experience deceiving secret affairs. It is important for Scorpio to understand the fear of not finding or keeping true love. Your male or female friend born in November does understand that beauty is not only physical but also spiritual. In order to experience true emotional and physical love, a well-balanced and harmonious relationship is the key.

Astropsychology Profile Sagittarius

Let's now explore souls born in December. Jupiter is the ruler of this fiery sign and will offer your friends born in December a philosophical and positive approach to life. Sagittarius will travel the world and channel Jupiter's teaching power constructively. Jupiter rules the Indians, the wild, foreign land, foreigners, Spain, Portugal, and Australia. The opportunity to regenerate the spirit is given through learning, teaching, and traveling.

Sagittarius, House Number 1

The soul's purpose of your friends born in December is to throw his arrows in the Universal Mind and explore the secret of the stars. These souls will have to travel the world around and be challenged by foreigners who are from different cultures and follow specific philosophies. Sagittarius is ruled and controlled by Jupiter, called in Greek mythology the "The Truth Seeker." Sagittarius rules also education, the codification of thoughts and knowledge amassed in books and seen as higher laws. The young Sagittarius soul will not challenge the books and turn himself into a professional student of dogmatic teachings. The advanced Sagittarius intuitively knows that the laws of the past do not apply any longer for our present generation and limit the progress of the soul. Thus, Sagittarius realizes the importance in rewriting the books with a more advanced knowledge that fit nowadays standards. Your friend born in December was born to explore new physical and spiritual horizons and communicate the findings. Sagittarius has a strong desire for freedom and exploration and will not jump into a relationship unless their independence is respected. As a rule Sagittarius attracts foreigners and many live in foreign lands. Your male or female friend born in December may look much younger than they really are. This rule does apply to any sign of the zodiac, especially if the person was born with a Moon or a Dragon's Head or Tail in Sagittarius/Gemini. Sagittarius gets bored easily and needs plenty of space to operate. This sign rules wide-open space, traveling, teaching, law, pets, the Indians and they need plenty of challenges. They are particularly good at teaching, and if they discipline themselves early enough they can become fantastic writers or prominent speakers.

Sagittarius, House Number 2

Let's explore the financial prospect and the attitude with money for those born in December. Look at House Number 2 in the Section Housing System and read the keywords to get more information. In this House, Sagittarius becomes a calculated Capricorn. Remember you can also refer to the Sun Sign Characteristics section and read more about Capricorn. Saturn rules this House and as a rule this karmic planet will not bring about riches without planning and hard work. Capricorn rules the government, engineering, structure and honor. Thus, many souls born in December may decided to work for a large corporation or Uncle Sam. Some prefer to operate in the Army or the Navy to satisfy their strong desire to travel to foreign lands. Your male or female friend born in December is a natural born communicator and many are using the latest technology to guide people and machines to their target. Others make money working in real estate, hotels, and restaurants. The advanced Sagittarius will spend time and money to obtain a higher education, and may wish to become a lawyer or a powerful financial businessman. The speed and swift thinking they were born with is the perfect tool needed to talk and service the people around them. Always concerned with money, your male or female Sagittarius friend may even be stingy or manipulative towards others. However, Saturn is watching them and will certainly bring a heavy karma to the unaware soul. Also, because the future is the reincarnation of the thoughts, if one wants to become a millionaire, one must talk and feel like a millionaire. The advanced Capricorn is a natural metaphysician, as represented by the head of the goat, or evil by Christian standards. Thus, the fish tail of the goat must be used wisely in relationship to the Universal tide produced by the Moon's fluctuations. More on this law is to be found in my book, ***The Power of the Dragon.***

Sagittarius, House Number 3

The 3rd House, rules the thinking process, and in this House your friend born in December becomes a freedom oriented Aquarius. Read House Number 3 in the Section Housing System and understand the keywords to get more information. Remember you can also refer to the Sun Sign Characteristics and read all about Aquarius. This advanced intellectual sign gives Sagittarius a vision for the future and a strong need to travel the world. Any Sagittarius soul will always shine through with his natural ability to attract others into his unique teaching powers. The young Sagittarius soul cannot think, see, or judge for himself; and becomes a walking talking book. The soul lost the spirit in the dogmatic printed words. Chances are that your local priest or religious leader was born in December or has a strong Dragon's Head or Tail in Sagittarius. The advanced Sagittarius does realize his own intellectual limitations; and through new studies and traveling will work hard to eliminate any archaic teachings. If Jupiter is badly aspected in anyone's chart, spiritual pride and total religious fanaticism is usually present. However, your Sagittarius friend does mean well; and in time may expand their cosmic consciousness. Aquarius rules the future, astrology, electronics; and this sign is unique, independent and futuristic in many ways. Thus, your male or female friend born in December may become a pilot, a computer wiz, an inventor or a precise Astropsychologist. Aquarius rules the fate of mankind for the next 2000 years, thus, children born nowadays were born with Pluto(death/regeneration) in Sagittarius (religion/law). Those children were born to completely restructure all religions as practiced today. A much more advanced generation of new spiritual leaders will ultimately end up in the deceiving age of Pisces and help mankind to realize its direct relationship with the universe as a whole. The mind of a Sagittarius is unique, and Uranus (ruler of Aquarius) gives them the incredible potential to master the secret of the stars and see into eternity.

Sagittarius, House Number 4

So now let's look in House Number 4 for those born in December. In the home area, your male or female Sagittarius friend becomes a soft Pisces. Refer to House Number 4 in the Section Housing System and read the keywords to get more information. Remember you can also refer to the Sun Sign Characteristics and read all about this Sun Sign. Pisces is an emotional and religious sign and many Sagittarius' are brought up with holy teachings. The young Sagittarius soul will travel far looking for a deity or a guru and embrace many different religious doctrines. The negative fish may also induce deceptions and stress produced by a family member's sickness, drug or alcohol abuse or intense religious poisoning. The young Sagittarius soul will make a mission to travel far away places and promote his specific religious doctrines and many build and live in churches. Pisces means healing the spirit and unselfishly helping others, thus, the advanced Sagittarius will use his home base for spiritual endeavors and guidance without the rigid, righteous religious attitudes. Neptune "The Lord of the Seas" rules this dreamy sign and many Sagittarius' will chose to live by the water or in an exotic place. Pisces rules the arts and the subconscious and your male or female friend born in December needs to spend time alone to become creative. Subsequently, many of them are great painters. They need to have water around them or surround themselves with spiritual, artistic or religious bits and pieces collected in the many trips around the world. If born with an afflicted moon or Dragon's Tail, those born in December are strongly advised to stay clear from alcohol and drugs and many are prone to drowning. Pisces also rules painting, photography and chemicals, thus, many Sagittarius' will have to use caution in handling or using the dangerous substances. Your male or female friend born in December will use the imaginative power of Neptune (ruler of Pisces) and become writers, artists, philosophers or religious leaders. Incidentally, Nostradamus was born in December and he used Pisces' power of the subconscious to foresee and write his famous prophecies from his home in Salon De Provence, France. Pisces rules water and clearly denunciates why the great Prophet use to glance at the water to transport himself in time and space using remote viewing to "see" the future. More on Nostradamus' life and his great astrological chart is in my book *The Power of the Dragon*.

Sagittarius, House Number 5

Let's now look at how someone born in December behaves or feels about love. In the love area, your male or female Sagittarius friend becomes an aggressive Aries. Look at House Number 5 in the Section Housing System and read the keywords and get more information. Remember you can also refer to the Sun Sign Characteristics and read all about the Aries Sun Sign. In the 5th House of love, romance and children, your friends or acquaintances born in December will attract those had born in August, February or April, they are also fond of those born in June. This is also the House of speculations and Aries rules action, speed, danger and competition. This is why many male souls born in December are attracted to dangerous or violent sports. The young Sagittarius soul will also compete and collect as many lovers as possible. Aries rules the head or the strong desire to find oneself, thus, the wiser Sagittarian female regenerates with education and will concentrate on a more intellectual partner who can stimulate her great mind. Those born in December are extremely curious about the people they deal with and once the mental stimulation is gone they are on to someone more interesting. Remember Sagittarius rules foreigners and philosophy. Many souls born in December are a magnet to these people. This sign rules the Indians and many of them thrive in equestrian activities while others enjoy mechanics and the speed and joy of cars. Being an Aries in the area of love and romance, the young soul born in December will behave like a child with love. Many of them will have to learn the hard way by suffering much heartache. Usually, once the competitive edge is burnt out and respect is offered, Sagittarius finds true love during the later part of their life. This sign is also gifted with computers, writing, traveling, and photography, public speaking, publishing and drawing. Souls born in December are shockingly honest with love and they all are looking for a true copy of themselves in someone else. Sadly enough the real soul mate is very rare, and difficult to find if at all, and once again Sagittarius is on the search. Because the mixture of this Fifth House, ruled by Aries (Germany) and Sagittarius (Latino), your male or female friend born in December will have to explore these countries or learn these languages. Many of these souls are great teachers, astrologers, and are futuristic; ultimately they are looking for themselves and others in this speculative House. They love the outdoors, sports, and action and will share it all with all the children of the world.

Sagittarius, House Number 6

Now let's look at House Number 6 and see how your male or female friend born in December behaves or feels about servicing the world and his health. In the work area, your male or female Sagittarius friend becomes a solid Taurus. Refer to the keywords to understand this House better. Taurus rules money and the banking industry, massage, the arts, music, singing, and also cosmetology. Taurus rules everything to do with spas, wealthy and classy environments, and everything to do with beauty. Now remember, Taurus (ruled by Venus) will motivate the soul to operate in a beautiful or artistic environment. Thus, many Taurus' will make money in the world of travel, communication, sales, publishing, or even writing. This is possible because Mercury naturally rules this 6th House. Sagittarius rules traveling the world, while Taurus means money, thus, your Sagittarius friend will be attracted to any job involving transportation. Taurus also rules wealth, thus, any endeavor involving communication or teaching will always pay off to a Sagittarius. The cosmetologist or singer is a good example to represent the mercurial creativity in your male or female friend born in December. Because Taurus is an earth sign, many Sagittarius' will cruise the world to extract wealth or investigate the behavior of mother earth. A geologist or gemologist is also a good illustration to represent an earthy Taurus sign on the 6th House cusp of work and service to the world. Because Taurus is a wealth and peace loving sign, the working environment can play an important part of your male or female friend's health. Thus, many Sagittarius' work as massage therapists in wealthy, classy spa environments. In the medical aspect of Astropsychology, Taurus rules the neck, and under stress, your male or female friend born in December may suffer neck or throat problems. Lastly, the keyword for Taurus is, "I have and I possess," thus, it is important for Sagittarius to let go of unhealthy working environments in order to improve their health.

Sagittarius, House Number 7

So now let's explore House Number 7 for those born in December. In the home area, your male or female Sagittarius friend becomes a dual Gemini. Look at House Number 7 in the Section Housing System and read the keywords to get more information. Remember you can also refer to the Gemini Sun Sign Characteristics and read all them. On the 7th House of marriage and business partnerships, souls born in December will attract those born in June, August and April, especially foreigners. This sign rules communication and indicates the true potential to become a speaker, writer, teacher, philosopher or a publisher. Souls born in December will want to travel the world, and they are quite lucky with foreign people. Many people born in December will end up marrying a an individual from a foreign country. Your male or female friend born in December is very spiritual, and the power to teach is shared through the communicative 7th House in Gemini. Because Mercury is an intellectual, dual planet, those born in December strive for learning and teaching philosophy. The advanced December souls love the stars, and many Sagittarius' also teach the laws of the universe. Gemini rules also photography, telephone work, newspapers, transportation, translation and sales. Those born in December have an inner ability to adapt to others and many will work hard to further one's education. On the negative aspect, as Mercury rules duality, many young souls born in December will experience two or four marriages. Gemini's symbol is the twin or a man and a woman. The challenge is set for them to experience the duality of Gemini, and the need for mental stimulation in all relationships. Your male or female friend born in December might have to speak a different language and live in a foreign land. The numbers 2, 4, 6, 8 etc. will follow them always throughout their long life.

Sagittarius, House Number 8

So now lets look in House Number 8 for those born in December. In the area of life and death, legacy, metaphysics and corporate money, your male or female Centaur friend becomes a soft Cancer. Read House Number 8 in the Section Housing System and get more awareness. Remember you can also refer to the Sun Sign Characteristics and read all about Cancer's Sun Sign. The Moon rules Cancer, thus your Sagittarius friend will be concerned about feeding and protecting his family and the world at large. Many December souls flourish in real estate, or work or run hotels, restaurants or become contractors/builders. The advanced ones concentrate on building up a solid spiritual knowledge so that they can feed families with spiritual knowledge and in the process establish financial security for themselves. Because Cancer rules properties and the 8th House legacy, your male or female friends born in December may inherit a house or in some case a hotel or a restaurant. The Moon rules the sign of Cancer and the 8th House rules insurance; thus, your old Sagittarius friend is concerned about his family and will make sure that all is taking care after his demise. This House rules also managing and distributing resources and many Sagittarius' are into managing other people's finances. Souls born in December do also work for large corporations even Uncle Sam, thus, many will operate within a high structured environment. Cancer is very shrewd in business and many Sagittarius' build financial towers for themselves and those they care. They are attracted and invest in valuable properties or help others to get a

I Know All About You 163

well-deserved retirement plan from the government. Because the Moon rules Cancer, any endeavor in this particular House should be handled in respect of the Moon's fluctuations for better results. This is also the House of death and indicates a long life and caring assistance from loved ones during the last part of life on this world. Because Cancer is a very spiritual sign, many advanced December souls feed guide and protect the world with their incredible psychic powers. The young Sagittarius soul may display a subconscious fear to expand outside of religious doctrines and invest time and money to preach conventional teaching.

Sagittarius, House Number 9

So now let's look in House Number 9 for those born in December. In the area of traveling, teaching, higher education and foreigners, your male or female friend born in December becomes a shining Leo. Leo is ruled by the Sun or the option to gather and promote the light is offered to the soul. Leo means total commitment to a purpose and teaching children, and with it the potential to reach a form of fame or respect. Leo rules notoriety and in the 9th House of foreign affairs and publishing your male or female friend born in December will get lucky in those areas. Leo rules also love and the opportunity given to Sagittarius to fall in love with a foreign person and reside in a foreign country. Many a Sagittarius will travel the world looking for the light and many will educate themselves by interacting with others. The more artistic Sagittarian will learn an art and operate in a foreign country. Studying music or philosophy will be rewarding to them and in the process your male or female friend born in December will get published and gain a good career position. Leo rules children, the stage and the arts and everything to do with fame. Thus, many Sagittarius' will find themselves teaching children physically or spiritually. Many of them are also masters in communication and in helping delinquent children to get back on the right track in life. Being so concerned and original in the House of teaching, many Sagittarius will travel far in body, mind and spirit to heal others. The advanced Sagittarius soul takes on studies involving the human mind or Astropsychology. The desire to bring light to others and explore unconventional disciplines is very strong. Others turn themselves into great explorers or inventors. You can be sure that, as Leo rules love and friends, that your male or female friend born in December will have contacts all over the world. This Jupiter driven spirit likes to travel far for the purpose of learning and teaching, and many work for well-established corporations passing on their valuable knowledge. Others will follow the Leo impulse and may become proficient teachers, speakers or famous writers. Friends born in April and October will also share the same desire to explore as your male or female friend born in December. Intellectual stimulation is important for any Sagittarius and they will quickly lose interest with those less inquisitive than they are. As a rule, those souls will regenerate by communicating, traveling, learning and teaching the children of the world.

Sagittarius, House Number 10

So now let's explore House Number 10 or the area of career and the public standing for those born in December. In that section of life, your male or female Sagittarius friend becomes a precise Virgo. Look at House Number 10 in the Section Housing System and read the keywords

I Know All About You

and get more information. Remember you can also refer to the Sun Sign characteristics and read all about the Virgo Sun Sign. The sign of Virgo rules organization, paper work, office work, the medical field, homeopathic medicine and plants. Thus, souls born in December are very precise and dedicated to their chosen profession. Many work also as editors, writers, and all that is needed to organize and clean the environment. They do enjoy a lot of mental activity and are adept in teaching children anything and everything about the world around them. Virgo also rules the medical field and many souls born in December strive to heal others and become nurses. The desire to provide and organize others through their career endeavor is very strong, and many Sagittarius' will work hard to raise money, and will participate in volunteer work. Because Mercury rules Virgo, your male or female friend born in December may also enjoy photography and become a writer or reporter for a large newspaper or famous magazine. Attractive souls born in December will also have the opportunity to get photos of themselves placed in magazines. The advanced Sagittarius soul will become a proficient speaker and will promote good health habits. The young souls will fall for the "Virgin Mary" religious pull; and impose dogmatic doctrines to the God fearing masses. Others may turn themselves into priests and further a specific organized religion. The desire to promote purity in body, mind and spirit, through the "Virgin Mary"(Virgo 10th House of career) area is very strong. Thus, many Sagittarian souls will feel compelled to travel the world and will do so. Because Virgo is an intellectual and very creative sign, your male or female friend born in December may gain recognition as a teacher or as a writer. Because Sagittarius rules the codification of thoughts, teaching, and books, it is important for them to keep an open and critical mind and challenge all printed material. Mercury (the ruler of Virgo) may also lead many of his children to work in law, bookstores, the telecommunications industry, or a telephone company.

Sagittarius, House Number 11

So now let's explore House Number 11 and see how your Sagittarius friend behaves with his friends. In that section of life, your male or female December friend becomes a diplomatic Libra. So now let's look at House Number 11 in the Section Housing System and read the keywords and get more information. Remember you can also refer to the Libra Sun Sign characteristics and read all of it. In the area of wishes and friends, those born in December will attract those born in October and April. So those born in those months have the potential to bring Sagittarius their wishes. Libra rules the law, justice, conventional psychology, Astropsychology, group organization, balance, and harmony. Thus, once Sagittarius refines himself and become a diplomatic Libra with others, the potential is then offered to reach many of his wishes. Libra is a very sensitive and artistic sign, thus, your advanced Sagittarius friend is a master of adaptation with many of his friends. Because Libra rules also marriage and contracts, Sagittarius will involve friends with his business and could end up marrying a long lasting friend. Your male or female friend born in December loves to communicate and could spend hours talking stars or metaphysics with others. It is important for your wallet and your time to tell your Sagittarius friend to get to the point. Because Sagittarius rules foreign lands, chances are that your male or female friend born in December will have friends from all over the world. However, don't expect them to take the time to sit down and write long letters, they would prefer the use of the telephone or the Internet. However, the location of the Moon or the Dragon's Head and Tail could intensify or diminish the communication gift. Venus rules Libra, and this sign rules also the arts. Thus, many of your Sagittarian friends will be involved in the arts, government, or be a mediator in some form. The desire for balance and harmony is also very strong, and your male or female friend born in December will compromise to keep harmony at all costs. Other planets positive or negative in this House denote the type of friends or wishes pursued by the subject.

Sagittarius, House Number 12

So now let's explore House Number 12 and see how your Sagittarius friend behaves subconsciously. In that section of the human experience, your male or female friend born in December becomes a powerful Scorpio. Look at House Number 12 in the Section Housing System and read the keywords to get more understanding. Remember you can also refer to the Scorpio characteristics and read all about this Sun Sign. Scorpio rules investigation, metaphysics, the medical field and high science, thus, your Sagittarius friend is a natural investigator of the unknown. The advanced December soul constantly regenerates in reading, learning or teaching deep metaphysical or medical studies. The Young Sagittarius soul will only nurture and promote archaic or religious teachings and may become fanatic in the process. However, Scorpio is also the sign of decay, life, and death; and will force the soul to rise above the printed words and reach the true spirit. Another downfall of this Plutonic position is the Scorpion's poisonous stinger or jealousy, resentment, revenge, and their inability to let go of a bad experience. As seen in Nostradamus' case, the great Prophet did rise from his rigid religious upbringing induced by his Jewish family into the unlimited cosmic consciousness and the old science of astrology. In any case, never forget that in the subconscious level, your Sagittarius friend could be a resentful Scorpio. Thus, subconsciously motivated, the nasty Scorpion stinger, in time and in space can reach you and do serious damage. The advanced ones are fully aware of this power and the karma it could generate against oneself. Scorpio rules also sex, others peoples resources, insurance, metaphysics, life and death. This subconscious motivation is very strong in the Sagittarius make up, and he or she will always gain more knowledge to reach full power and full control in one or many areas involving the affairs of this House. Much of the best research or deep study is often accomplished in secret then used for the good of mankind. Of course any planet in the 12th House will also play an important part of its subconscious motivation. Much more can be divulged especially in my book **The Power of the Dragon**. Because the subconscious is somehow deceiving, your male or female friend born in December may have a conflict between physical possession and spiritual knowledge. Many will be able to get the true knowledge they are striving for.

Astropsychology Profile Capricorn

Let us move on now and explore those born in January. Those born in the wintertime have a long and arduous mountain to climb against the wind, the cold, and the snow. Calculating Saturn is the ruler of this earthy sign and in time he will always reward his children, and give them a high position in life where money, power, and organization rule.

Capricorn, House Number 1

The soul's purpose of your friends born in January is to establish a solid career where respect and recognition and power will be offered sometime late in life. Caring and spiritual, the advanced Capricorn will build a tower where he can coordinate, feed and protect his family and the world at large. This sign has a fish tail and denotes the importance for your male or female friend born in January to be aware and use the Moon's fluctuations in his business affairs. Young souls born in January can be extremely rational even skeptical to anything unproved scientifically. Doing so can slow down the higher purpose they are to accomplish on earth. Realizing that what they do not see or understand just yet, doesn't mean it cannot exist. This attitude produces scientists or astronomers who explore the Universal Mind rationally, casting aside the precious spiritual values of the stars. At this point in his reincarnation, the young January soul cannot enter the intuitional domain of the stars and might not be allowed to gain cosmic consciousness in this lifetime. The more advanced ones are a recipient of wisdom and awareness, and will make good use of the Universal Mind's secrets for the well being of the world. Capricorn rules the government, structuring, planning, power, politics and large organizations. The head of the Goat was subconsciously chosen by Christianity to represent evil. There is nothing evil in your male or female friend born in January, as the real evil is ignorance. Religious people are reluctant to let go of the past and dogmas, while Capricorn is the engineer and the architect of the zodiac who builds cities and the future. Capricorn rules mathematics and structural projects. On the negative aspect, the young Capricorn scientist soul also builds nuclear bombs leading to the destruction of civilization as perceived by many religious organizations. On a very negative side, dictators such as Hitler and Joseph Stalin were born with a negative Dragon in Capricorn and he used and abused the power of structural Saturn. But Saturn is a karmic planet and in due time, always crashes down the soul and his pyramid of manipulation. Incidentally, many world and United States Presidents were born with a strong Capricorn in their chart.

Capricorn, House Number 2

Let's now explore the House of money and self-esteem for those born in January. Look into House Number 2 and the Sign of Aquarius. Now your male or female friend

I Know All About You 171

born in January becomes an Aquarius when dealing or making money. Remember you can also refer to the Houses or the Sun Sign Characteristics and read all about Aquarius. Aquarius rules electronics, television, radio, aeronautics, the New Age, Astrology and anything to do with hi-tech. Thus, Capricorn will be forced by the Universal Mind to dwell with electronics in some ways to make money. Capricorn is a genius when it comes to hi-tech and many work very closely with it. Because Aquarius rules also astrology and Astropsychology, Capricorn may secretively investigate his relationship with the universe and invest in the stars. A famous TV host such as Oprah Winfrey and modern astrologer Jane Dixon made good use of their Second House of money in Aquarius. Understand that the Astropsychology that I have created is from a far more accurate and simpler way than any astrological work produced previously by many famous writers; and I'll let you be the judge of that! Aquarius means also freedom and traveling the world, thus, your male or female friend born in January will travel by air far and fast. Remember Capricorn rules politics, and well-known political figures do fly all over the world non-stop to represent their country or to dwell with a myriad of emergency situations. Capricorn is a very structural sign, thus, as induced by the 2nd House of income in the sign of Aquarius, many make money this way. Your male or female friend born in January will travel the world electronically and invest in the latest state of the art electronics to do so. Some will take chances with the stock market, which is another Aquarius manifestation on this dense physical world. The World Wide Web or the Internet is also a way for your Capricorn friend to free himself from the boundary of his home and experience the world the Aquarius way. Japan is an Aquarius country and many successful and powerful Capricorn executives will be attracted by this part of the world. Other smart January souls start their own skyscraper businesses and start their own multi-level endeavors. Because Aquarius rules friends, many Capricorns will involve their close friends in their moneymaking schemes.

Capricorn, House Number 3

Let's now investigate the Pisces 3rd House of communication for those born in January. Remember to refer to the Housing System and the Sun Sign Characteristics and read all about Pisces. The 3rd House, rules the thinking process, thus, your friend born in January becomes a Pisces. Because Neptune rules the introverted sign of Pisces, souls born in January may not talk as much as you do. You will often catch them daydreaming or lost in the past. Understand that Pisces is a water sign and the moon affects all water signs. Thus, after the full moon, work a little harder to take your male or female friend born in January out of the blue before getting into a deep depression. Also, Pisces rules drugs and alcohol, and those born in January are strongly advised to stay clear away from any and all chemicals. The addiction will blur Capricorn's mental faculty and induce severe depressions that could lead the soul into a mental institution. Neptune rules the subconscious; thus, many Capricorn souls are extremely intuitive and are attracted to the subtle mystery of life. The young souls may follow negative fish, and the will of this sign has produced corrupted Capricorn evangelists named Oral Roberts and the organized religious promoter, Jim Baker. The wiser souls will use their inner psychic ability to guide others in life or turn their imaginative minds to music, dancing and/or photography. Capricorn can also create in

I Know All About You 173

the minds eye and crystallize his thoughts under the form of books while others will work hard on movie productions. Because Pisces is an artistic sign, your male or female friend born in January will appreciate and feel music like no other sign of the zodiac. On the negative aspect, as Pisces rules imagination, those born in January may suffer unfounded health or spiritual fears. However, Capricorn is born a visionary, and the power to see the future for himself and those he cares for is quite accurate and will materialize in time. The mind of your male or female Capricorn friend is over-sensitive to the thoughts of others. Pisces rules this House of communication and this sign will make them intuitive, soft-spoken and caring to all. As always, the Moon's fluctuations will play an important part of your male or female friend born in January; and being aware of this phenomenon would help them to understand and control depression.

Capricorn, House Number 4

Let's move on to the 4th House and investigate it. In the home area, your male or female Capricorn friend becomes an Aries. So now let's look at House Number 4 in the Section Housing System and read the keywords and get more information. Remember you can also refer to the Sun Sign Characteristics and read all about Capricorn. Aries is ruled by the fiery, even dangerous planet Mars. You can be sure that your male or female friends born in January will treat every one of his family members equally. However, the Goat could also use his sharp horns if anyone endangers his family or his security. It is common for those born in January to have a workshop and sharp tools at home. Your male or female friend born in January loves to use their engineering talent at home and could also suffer cuts or burns by fixing appliances. Because Mars rules flames, it is important for them to insure the house against fire. Aries is born to be a leader and combined with the structural power of Capricorn, souls born in January want to be the first ones to create something original. Later in life, this aptitude is often used in mechanical or engineering work. Many inventors and chemistry geniuses were born in January and many ended up blowing up their house. Remember Mars rules war and danger, thus, ammunition and weapons should be secured in parts of the house away from the children. At a tender age, souls born in January are daredevils; Mars (the planet of action and danger) usually induces cuts, stitches and broken bones. For the more advanced Capricorn, the urgency and leadership power of Mars will be used on a mental plane. Thus, the opportunity to initiate and lead any communication endeavor may bring the soul towards operating on the radio or writing. Because of the impatience generated by Mars, your male or female friend born in January may also become quite harsh or demanding at home and this could bring friction with close family members. The strong desire to lead and control all areas of the home life could also hinder Capricorn's desire for harmony and a peaceful home life. However, the universe is offering those born in January to initiate, lead, organize and structure their career right from the base of operation. Thus, your male or female Capricorn friend may find it hard to relax and need to get away from home, especially if he or she operates a business from home. Like the Goat, Aries is a mountain sign and they do strive to establish a home in the peaceful surrounding of a high mountain.

Capricorn, House Number 5

Let's now look at how a Capricorn behaves or feels about love, romance and children. So now let's look in House Number 5 for those born in January, refer to House Number 5 in the Section Housing System and master the keywords. In the love area, your male or female Capricorn friend becomes a Taurus. In the 5th House of love and romance and children, your friends born in January will attract those born in May and September while a Cancer will always be a magnet to them. Venus (the planet of love, arts and beauty) rules this elegant and sophisticated sign. Thus, Capricorn strives to establish a long lasting commitment with someone who must be spiritually or physically beautiful and has the potential to make money. This House rules also speculation and Taurus loves music, singing and all the refined things in life. Thus, do not expect to find your male or female friend at a rock concert, unless he or she was born with a wild moon in a fire sign. Instead, look for them at the theater or anywhere where wealth, power, classical music or a high form of art is expressed. As Venus rules beauty, the children of a Capricorn are usually gifted, smart and often very attractive. Because Taurus is the sign of wealth, your male or female friend born in January wants his children to marry well and will provide only the best for their education. This is the House of love, romance, and children; thus, like a fierce buffalo, your male or female friend born in January will be extremely possessive and protective of his children. The strong motivation to do more than the best for the children always produces a well-balanced and well-disciplined youngster. Taurus loves luxury, good food, candlelight and most of all solidity in love. Sadly enough many signs of the zodiac do not match the high expectations of your Capricorn friend and many do suffer distressing heartbreaks in life. Your male or female friend born in January will speculate and try to make money at what he or she loves to do most. Stubborn and persistent they usually succeed late in life, especially in the love area. They usually are attracted to older people when young and much younger as they get older. The partner is usually attractive and has the potential to rise to his own place in the social ladder.

Capricorn, House Number 6

Now we will look at House Number 6 in the Section Housing System to see how your male or female friend born in January behaves or feels about health and servicing the world. In the work area, your male or female Capricorn friend becomes a Gemini. Remember you can also refer to the Sun Sign Characteristics and read all about this Sun Sign. This is the House of work, and as Gemini is an intellectual sign, your male or female friend born in January becomes a communicator. Mercury rules Gemini and Mercury rules communication, sales, writing and indeed the radio world. The advanced soul born in January will become a "Messenger of the Gods," and during the course of his life will reach millions of people passing invaluable information to the masses. Incidentally, famous radio and TV hosts such as Jeff Rense, Rush Limbaugh, Howard Stern and Dr. Laura were all born in January. On the medical aspect of Astropsychology, this sign rules the arms and hands. Thus, we can see the swiftness of speed and accuracy in two famous Capricorn boxers, Mohammed Ali and George Foreman. Gemini rules also communication, photography and magazines. Vendela, a Capricorn, is not only a famous model but she also speaks

I Know All About You

five different languages fluently. Kate Moss, also a Capricorn, is another example of a famous model known internationally. You will find Capricorn's working anywhere from driving taxis, working in telecommunications, transcribing legal papers, or as the chief executive officer of a large corporation. The job is to talk, sell, adapt, travel, photograph, report, write, and a myriad of other occupation's demanding a swift mind and the gift of organization. Mercury is fast and adaptable. Also, it may send the soul to work at a junkyard for many arduous years, or build a race car so he can compete, or establish a position of respect in society. Your male or female friend born in January was blessed by the Universal Mind with the faster tools and a super aptitude to adapt and serve the world in any Mercurial way he chooses. The 6th House is also the House of health, and Gemini rules the respiratory system. Thus, under stress allergies may develop and could become a serious problem for Capricorn. Gemini rules the hands and fingers and many souls born in January are prone to break bones, especially driving fast around town.

Capricorn, House Number 7

So now let's look in House Number 7 for those born in January and see how and with whom your male or female friend faces the world. In the partnership area, your friend becomes a Cancer. On the 7th House of Marriage and business partnerships, souls born in January will attract those born in July, September and May. Cancer is the sign of home, family, security and food. Many of them will be attracted to those whom in some way feed and protect the public. Sometimes a close family member owns or run this type of business. In facing the world, your Capricorn friend will be super sensitive, intuitive and caring. Because

Cancer is water (feminine sign) those born in January will be quite shy and introverted, unless of course, they inherited a powerful fiery moon or an aggressive Dragon. Your male or female friend born in January is looking for a long-standing relationship with someone willing to take on all the challenges to assure a solid marriage. Capricorn will not get involved with just anybody. This sign is attracted to status, position, and needs respect in the eyes of the world. The 7th House also deals with contracts, and as the moon rules Cancer, those souls must understand and respect the Moon's fluctuations before making a long lasting commitment. Family matters and children are extremely important for the Goat, and many will do all they can to assure the best in education for their offspring. Because Capricorn rules power, and old age, your male or female friend born in January will attract older souls while young and much younger as they get older. The desire to feed and protect others is quite strong, thus, as induced by the stars, many younger souls in need will be attracted to their position, power and money. Capricorn knows that success and notoriety don't come easy, however, they will always help those willing to work hard to climb the long rocky mountain. Sometimes, as seen in Hitler's fate, the goat misuses his political planning powers; subsequently, creating a long and painful fall induced by Saturn, their karmic ruler. (See my book, ***The Power of the Dragon***, to learn more about the fate of famous and infamous people.)

Capricorn, House Number 8

Let us now see what is going on in House Number 8 for those born in January. In the area of life and death, legacy, metaphysics and corporate money, your male or female

Capricorn friend becomes a Leo. So now let's look at House Number 8 in the Section Housing System and read the keywords and get more information. Remember you can also refer to the Sun Sign Characteristics and read all about this Sun Sign. Because Leo, the ruler of this House rules children, Capricorn will always be concerned with the after-life and affairs of the dead. This House deals with legacy, and Capricorn is very concerned with what will happen to his family after his departure from this world. Leo is also the sign of fame, thus, those born in January do attract those who have or can make a significant amount of money. This sign also rules the arts, and your male or female friend born in January will perceive and invest in the artistic abilities of his children. This House deals with death, but as Leo is the sign of life, many Capricorn's live a very long life. As a rule, the first part of a Capricorn's life is very challenging, but Saturn will always reward them, especially towards the end of their existence. Leo rules the heart, thus, it is important for Capricorn to take time off from the daily challenges of life and avoid serious heartaches. However, no matter how life treats them, even after the dissolution of a marriage, Capricorn will always provide for their child. A successful Capricorn will spend much of his time raising money for the welfare of the children of the world. This House also deals with corporate money, thus, your male or female friend born in January will attract and perform with talented and wealthy people. Leo, the sign of love, rules France and Italy; thus, the wealthy Capricorn will also spend large amounts of money to acquire very expensive items from these countries. The potential to shine with the arts, children, and the business resources is offered to the January soul. Many of them also gain recognition after their death by leaving a beautiful legacy to the children. Many great writers of children's books, and television producers were born in January. The regeneration principle takes place when your male and female friend born in January promotes life and happiness for the children of tomorrow.

Capricorn, House Number 9

How does your Capricorn friend feel or behave in House Number 9? Look at House Number 9 and gather more information. This is the area of religion, traveling, learning, teaching, publishing and relationships with foreigners. In this area your Capricorn friend becomes a Virgo. Virgo is ruled by Mercury, or in Greek mythology "The Messenger of the Gods." Incidentally, Virgo is also the sign chosen by Christians to represent "The Virgin Mary," chastity, and perfection. The purpose of the "Virgin" is to take care of the "Temple of God" or the human body. Thus, your male or female friend born in January will be naturally in-tune to learn and teach health matters. Virgo rules the rainforest, plants and greenery, thus, more than any other sign; your male or female friend born in January will be very concerned with diet and especially vegetarianism. As seen with all zodiac signs, the positive and negative values of Virgo can be exaggerated and turn your Capricorn friend into a health freak. However, the desire for perfection and health is part of their powerful gift and may become a serious contribution to the world. Many successful physicians were born in January and their natural inclination for prescribing homeopathic medicine is a sure plus for this chemically poisoned world. The 8th House also deals with the wild or rural areas; thus, your Capricorn friend may decide to live high in the mountains, away from all the city pollution. This House also deals with foreign lands; thus, they will also attract and

I Know All About You 181

work with some foreigners, furthering the physical or spiritual health of the world. Virgo also rules clothing, thus, Capricorn thrives in fashion trading from one country to another. Because Virgo rules plants and greenery, many souls born in January do also very well from the products of the earth. The strong desire to learn and teach all about health and perfection is part of the Capricorn cosmic will, and without them, the world would be a very dirty and unorganized place to live.

Capricorn, House Number 10

Let's now get into House Number 10. This is the area of career, public standing, and accomplishments. In this area your male or female Capricorn friend becomes a very diplomatic Libra. Look at House Number 10 in the Section Housing System and read the keywords and get more information on this House. Remember you can also refer to the Sun Sign characteristics and read all about Libra Sun Sign. Venus or "The Queen of Love" in Greek mythology rules Libra. Thus, your male or female Capricorn friend has been given the opportunity to use Libra's diplomatic gift in his career. Venus means also the arts, gracious people, a lovely environment, and the power of establishing productive relationships. Thus, adapting to the harmonious sign of Libra, Capricorn is also attracted to interior designing, psychology, Astropsychology, or any endeavor demanding a sense of tact in the balance of energy. As seen again with Dr. Laura (a Capricorn) and John Gray (a Libra), both are in the field of communication, writing, and psychology. Incidentally Libra rules "the diplomat," and chances are that your male or female friend born in January is a part of your local government or works for the city or a large corporation. In the medical aspect of astrology, Libra rules the kidneys, and your Capricorn friend might be also prone to suffer allergies under stress or an unbalanced environment. However, Capricorn is always aware of his commitment to the country and his family and will do all he can to avoid unnecessary health risks. Your male or female friend born in January loves to deal or be seen with people who have gained power and a position of respect in their career. Libra rules justice, peace and harmony and this sign will not tolerate injustice in any form. The sign of peace can also declare war to bring about peace, balance and harmony to the world. A good representation of the justice principle of Libra is to be found with a Capricorn, or a government figure traveling to a country torn apart. The purpose of his mission is to reestablish harmony with other countries through diplomatic means, thus, stopping or avoiding war.

Capricorn, House Number 11

How does your male or female friend born in January feel or behave with his friends? This is the area of wishes, friends, and group organization. In this area, Capricorn becomes a powerful and secretive Scorpio. Look at House Number 11 in the Section Housing System and read the keywords and get more information. Remember you can also refer to the Sun Sign characteristics and read all about Scorpio. Pluto "The God of Hades" in Greek mythology rules this House and the sign of Scorpio. Knowing that Scorpio rules power, life and death, corporate money and investigation your male or female friend born in January will surely attract Plutonic type of friends. Often, in his research for a powerful position, the young Capricorn soul will make good use of those mighty friends, and would bring about serious karma to himself. It is easy to win the battle by eliminating your adversary before the rat race is started. Scorpio rules also investigation, sex, and secrets;

and with it the potential to expose others hidden endeavors to the world. The more advanced ones realize that without powerful friends no wish can be granted. They own their friend's respect and commitment by involving them in their business venture. Scorpio rules also metaphysical investigations, and many powerful government figures deal and consult psychics and astrologers in the secrecy of a friend's home. The Capricorn symbol is in itself a metaphysician, and is represented by Christians as the head of the goat or evil. Your male or female friend born in January strives for power, accomplishment, and respect from others. However, karmic Saturn is watching and will stop the young soul using and abusing others to gain recognition. In the worse case scenario, the soul is brought back to the ground and forced to rebuild it all honestly. Those born in November and May are the chosen friends of a Capricorn, while any other sign can also be attracted due to a hidden Moon in Taurus or a Dragon's Head or Tail in Scorpio in the chart. If the motivations are positive, a Capricorn's friend is a powerful channel for success. If not, the same friend can bring negative elements and bring about death and drama to the subject.

Capricorn, House Number 12

Let's now investigate what is going on in the subconscious area of your male or female friend born in January. So now let's look at House Number 12 in the Section Housing System and read the keywords and get more information. In this hidden area, Capricorn becomes a spiritual Sagittarius. This is the area of fear, imagination, the subconscious and deception. Sagittarius loves to study, thus, your male or female friend born in January will spend much time alone to do so. The subconscious desire to educate themselves is very strong as the gathered information may help the competitive Capricorn use the information to climb the mountain of success and recognition. It is also important for those born in January to realize that the books do not necessarily teach the truth. On a negative note, Neptune rules fears in this House of the subconscious. Thus, your Capricorn friend may nurture a subconscious fear to miss the ultimate information or education that will propel him to the top of the mountain of accomplishments. Sagittarius rules also the codification of thoughts, the law, foreign affairs, and much interest goes in that direction. Your Capricorn friend has a strong subconscious desire to be a part of history and to be remembered forever via the printed words and history books. Because Sagittarius rules education, your male or female friend born in January is also subconsciously motivated to enforce the world with the rules. This attitude can be exaggerated as seen with Dr. Laura's constant religious remarks on her syndicated radio show. The young Capricorn soul must understand that life is a constant process of changes and both the rules and the law are also changing. It is important for them to realize also how the Moon's fluctuations can affect their subconscious negatively and make them feel depressed.

Astropsychology Profile Aquarius

We are now ready to explore the chart of those born in February. Uranus, ruler of Aquarius gives your friends born in February the opportunity to master the secret of the Universal Mind and pass it on to the rest of the world. Aquarius is an air sign and, like the wind must travel the world and cannot be pinned down for long.

Aquarius, House Number 1

The soul's purpose of your friends born in February is to explore the incredible and make an intellectual impact in the world at large. Uranus (God of the Sky) in Greek mythology rules Aquarius, and many souls born in February must understand the importance of their mission on earth. The advanced Aquarius soul is always from the future and in time and space and reincarnated to advance the human spirit. Aquarius rules Universal Love, freedom, originality, inventions, aeronautics, the future of mankind, and astrology to name a few. Each and every planet in our solar system is both positive and negative, so are all of the Sun Signs. The downfall of this unusual sign is to misuse the eccentric forces of Uranus and become a rebel of all establishments. In the Chinese mythology, the Tiger is the chosen symbol to represent Aquarius. It is important for those born in February not to become overbearing, too bossy or self centered. Not all Aquarius' will behave this way though; a wise Moon or Dragon's Tail in any disciplined sign such as Capricorn or shy Virgo will always tone down the power of the wild Tiger. Aquarius rules all the children of the world and the potential to teach us all about mystical truths, and the stars. Thus, Aquarius is a true magnet to the children and will help them to reach the best of their potential. Uranus gives your male or female friend born in February enormous magnetism, originality, ingeniousness, and ultimately the power to reach fame and fortune during the course of this reincarnation. Uranus is quite exceptional in nature and may lead the soul to become or operate in an inimitable fashion. Due to the rareness of Uranus' personality and quality, those born in February will encounter incredible experiences. Incidentally, in my case, I was born in February and have experienced four solid UFO encounters. The soul's purpose of your Aquarius friend is usually reached in a weird and unpredictable way.

Aquarius, House Number 2

Let's now explore the House of money and self-esteem for those born in February. Look at House Number 2 in the Section Housing System and read the keywords and get more information. With money, your male or female friend born in February becomes a big-hearted and creative Pisces. Remember you can also refer to the Sign Characteristics and read all about Pisces Sun Sign. Aquarius rules the future while Pisces rules the subconscious, psychic work and the arts. Thus, many souls born in February are fine artists or precise spiritual leaders and natural Astropsychologists. While Aquarius rules television, computers, and cruising the world; Pisces rules illusion, music, photography, the medical field, oil, the oceans, and cinematography. Wherever Pisces is in a chart, there is total unselfishness and tremendous rewards for the lucky recipient or the spiritual student. Because Pisces is so giving of his natural spiritual gifts, the universe will always provide by bringing about good karma to the soul. On a negative note, the all-loving Pisces can get used and abused by inconsiderate souls, depleting both his financial and spiritual wealth. Pisces is a dreamy sign, and the trusting soul may not thoroughly look at all the fine lines of a contract; and stick himself in a bad deal. However, by magic and sometimes at the last minute the universe does provide and help the deserving soul. Pisces rules the subconscious and many advanced Aquarian soul's build their finances and self-esteem by providing spiritual help or furthering education for a living. Pisces is a water sign and is naturally ruled by the moon. Thus, the awareness and respect of the Moon's fluctuations can help the fish to swim upstream towards emotional, financial and spiritual stability. Many successful teachers and writers were also born in February and much of their endeavors are directed towards traveling and educating the children of the world.

Aquarius, House Number 3

The 3rd House, rules the thinking process and the assimilation of information and the communication power. In this House, your male or female friend born in February becomes a very competitive and impatient Aries. Look at

House Number 3 in the Section Housing System and read the keywords and get more information. Remember you can also refer to the Sun Sign characteristics and read all about the Aries Sun sign. Knowing that Aries rules competitiveness and innovation, Aquarius is extremely spirited, independent and aggressive intellectually. Thus, those born in February are strongly advised to learn to listen to others and practice verbal diplomacy. The Aries thinking process is so high-speed that Aquarius formulates both the questions and the answers almost immediately. A swift Moon in Gemini or a Dragon in another speedy air sign would make the thinking process as fast as lightning. Patience and learning to listen is strongly recommended in such a case. It is natural for an Aquarius soul to lead in all conversations and this egocentric attitude could bring conflict to a more passive or less competitive sign. Aquarius can gain much more by thinking and acting in a more sophisticated manner, especially in dealing with others. Aries rules the head and Mars (The Lord of War) rules this sign; thus, your male or female friend born in February was born to become a leader in his or her own right, especially where research, writing, teaching, the art, sports and innovation is concerned. The lifestyle, personality and accomplishments of these famous February souls is quite obvious; Peter Fonda, Princess Stephanie, Michael Jordan, Eva Gabor, Arsenio Hall, John Travolta, Oprah Winfrey, Garth Brooks, Burt Reynolds and of course, your spiritual teacher, Dr. Turi. The mind of an Aquarius is always concerned with the future, freedom, traveling, the Universal Light and indeed competitiveness in all fronts. Thus, Aquarius inherited the right mental recipe for success and will strive for the public eye. The young soul has much to learn about the childlike Aries mental attitude and might find it difficult to automatically analyze his

I Know All About You 189

verbal or physical actions against others. Be patient and be tolerant, they will need you to refine the Martian spirit to pass on their very important message to the world.

Aquarius, House Number 4

So now let's investigate House Number 4 for those born in February. In the home area, your male or female Aquarius friend becomes a solid Taurus. Investigate House Number 4 in the Section Housing System and read the keywords to gather more information. Remember you can also refer to the Sun Sign Characteristics and read all about Taurus. Because Taurus rules solidity, wealth, and the arts, your male or female friend born in February needs a beautiful home where power and wealth must be expressed. Taurus is a musical sign and many Aquarius' dream of having a piano and beautiful and expensive works of art. Because Taurus is the symbol chosen by the ancients to represent wealth, the option is given to those born in February to use the base of operations as a "bank," or run a very successful business right from the security of their home. Taurus rules also massage, expensive and elegant spas; thus, the option for any famous Aquarian is to enjoy or even live within the best of the best that money can afford anywhere in the world. Venus, the planet of love and art rules Taurus. This sign rules also singing; thus, many lucky February souls were born with artistic or wealthy parents (such as Princess Stephanie of Monte Carlo, John Travolta and Peter Fonda to name a few) and will explore their creativity early in life. However, regardless of their upbringing or early opportunities for success, your male or female friend born in February can and usually does rise to fame and fortune, and power, during the course of their tumultuous life. On a more spiritual side, some Aquarius souls willingly avoid physical fame and aim for a more refined way of life and concentrate on traveling and educating the world of its many wonders. As Aquarius rules Astrology and Astropsychology, many advanced February souls operate directly from their luxurious homes to teach the world the wonder of the stars. Your male or female friend born in February requires beauty and security in the total privacy of home where he or she can reach the Universal Mind or the deepest creative side of himself or herself. As a rule, the universe brings Aquarius a luxurious residence where spiritual power, fame, and money are used to bring forth the light to others. Intense and spiritual, some Aquarius souls will also work hard to preserve the beauty, and the wonder of nature.

Aquarius, House Number 5

Let's now look how an Aquarius behaves or feels about creativity, love, romance and children. Refer to House Number 5 in the Section Housing System and read the keywords to get more information. In the love area, your male or female Leo friend becomes a witty Gemini. Remember you can also refer to the Sun Sign Characteristics and read all about Gemini. In the 5th House of love and romance, your friends or acquaintances born in February will attract foreigners and those born in August, October, June and December. Mercury, "The Messenger of the Gods" rules Gemini, thus, your Aquarius friends will strive for knowledge and wisdom and may become a speaker or a writer. Mercury rules also magazines, languages, photography, broadcasting, and many Aquarius souls will reach fame and fortune in the field of communications. The Aquarius soul rules and thrives in the following endeavors: television, aeronautics, computers,

Astropsychology, astrology; and in any advanced, even weird topics such as UFOs, etc. Mercury rules also transportation, driving, telephone work, and journalism; thus, your male or female friend born in February will be attracted to those career options. The more advanced Uranian souls will perceive, master, and promote the future of mankind. Through this, your Aquarius friend is seen as an inventor or a promoter of the true Universal Light, as they are doing what they are supposed to master; thus, passing it on to the world. When dealing with love your male or female Aquarius friend needs mental stimulation and a very spiritual partner that can stimulate their powerful mind. Due to the dual impact of Gemini in the House of love, Aquarius will always attract two (or four) people at a time. This could prove distressing to a more fixed or emotional sign. Usually Aquarius produces twins or extremely sharp children. The passion and the flames of love of an Aquarius intensify constantly if the chosen partner is intellectually inclined and shares Aquarius' mission of truth. Aquarius always succeeds in life as a speaker, teacher or writer. Fame and the stage come naturally to the Water bearer, and the advanced soul is not afraid to share the light with a lucky and perceptive partner. The powerful light of their forward-thinking ruler (Uranus) belongs to them, and with the help of a worthwhile loving partner, must be shared to the world.

Aquarius, House Number 6

Let's see how your male or female friend born in February behaves or feels about health and servicing the world. In the work area, your male or female Aquarius friend becomes an emotional Cancer. Refer to House Number 6 in the Section Housing System and read the keywords for this House. By birth, your male or female friend born in February becomes a very sensitive and responsible soul. Cancer rules food, hotels, restaurants, real estate, home, families, and nature at large. Thus, your male or female friend born in February must feed and protect the world. Cancer rules also country music, and as seen with Garth Brooks. With Brooks, the feeding and protecting process is taking place by singing and feeding the world with passionate music. The same caring and protective attitude for families and the children of the world apply with well know February born actress, Elizabeth Taylor. The more practical Aquarius souls will run, operate, or own large and well-established real estate properties, famous spas, hotels and restaurants. This House deals also with health, and Cancer rules food and the stomach. Thus, your male or female friends born in February should avoid eating when upset. The moon also rules Cancer, and the young Aquarius soul may suffer serious depressions or setbacks if unaware of the Moon's fluctuations upon his health or service to the world. Cancer is a very emotional sign; thus, regardless of whatever service your male or female Aquarius friend is offering to the world, be sure of a total commitment and a will of steel to do so. Understanding, using, and respecting the moon or the ruler of this particular House is a must for Aquarius, as doing so can only bring about a strong, healthy and successful service to the world. Note: The United States of America (July 4th, 1776) is a Cancer country. Thus, America provides and supplies an extensive amount of food to families all over the world including their own. Also, no other country in the world produces that much food and spends so much money trying to lose weight. Thus, those born in February must avoid eating under stress and must keep physically active to stay strong and healthy. Wherever Cancer is located in your chart, the opportunity to feed and protect is given to you. Simply, make sure to respect the Universal Law of the Moon to rise to fame and power.

Aquarius, House Number 7

So now let's look in House Number 7 for those born in February and see how and with whom your male or female Aquarius friend faces the world. Refer to House Number 7 in the Section Housing System and read all the keywords to get more information. In the partnership area, your friend becomes a shining Leo. On the 7th House of Marriage and business partnerships, souls born in February will attract those born in August, June, December and October. Leo is a fire and fame oriented sign. This solar sign rules fame, the stage, children, light, the arts and all that means life itself. Thus, your male or female friend born in February will attract those unique partners that will have their own wealth or place in the sun. Aquarius will attract outstanding partners who were also born to offer light to the world. They do attract people who are original and have special physical or spiritual talents. It is very important for your male or female Aquarius friend to shine with the solar partner; thus, Aquarius will not accept less than extreme beauty and great talent for a long lasting relationship. Meantime, the advanced Aquarius soul knows also that beauty is not only physical but also spiritual. Beauty, title, education and money will play an important part of their choice but as a rule they will chose the mind and true love over anything else. Your Aquarius friend is a walking magnet facing the world and will never be short of their choice of incredible partners. Much of their spiritual growth will take place with those partners, as your male or female friend born in February cannot survive without love. As King of the zodiac or turning into Leo with a partner, Aquarius does expect and demand total loyalty and true commitment from those they have chosen. Anything less than special or a real Queen will turn the King into a ferocious wild beast ready to tear apart the unworthy offender. Listening to their head instead of their big heart is strongly recommended, as Leo is very committed and passionate in the affairs of love. Aquarius and his chosen unique royal partner will travel the world to further love and light to the world. The world will see this couple as unique, extremely magnetic with a very special message from the stars.

Aquarius, House Number 8

In the area of life and death, legacy, metaphysics, sex and corporate money, your male or female friend born in February becomes a Virgo, the "perfectionist." Refer to the Section Housing System and read the keywords to understand this House or this sign better. Virgo is a sign of health and will always be interested in the after-life and affairs of the dead. Because this sign rules discipline, service, and perfection; and because this is the House of sex, Aquarius will try all they can to satisfy their lover. This House also deals with legacy and Virgo is very conscious of what will happen to his family or the children of the world after his demise. Thus, much work will be done to make sure his valuable possessions are shared equally among members of his family. Because Virgo is an intellectual sign, your male or female Aquarius will not hesitate to offer portions of his resources to further health research and education. The sign of Virgo rules homeopathic medicine and the body of man. The 8th House rules corporate endeavors; thus, many Aquarians are involved with groups or generate revenue in the medical field or any line of spiritual regeneration work. Aquarius is a very unique sign, and as a rule, extremely curious, while Virgo is detail and health oriented. This House also deals with metaphysics, life and death, legacy, and in some ways how money will be generated from a business. This clearly denotes why many souls born in February are so concerned with life and death. The young and more practical Aquarius soul will become an astronomer, a computer wiz, an astronaut, an inventor, or will aim towards astrophysics. The more advanced soul will explore the secrets of life and death by investigating the spiritual values of the stars and uncover the secret of the Universal Mind. On a negative note, because of the rational and skeptical attitude of the earth element, Virgo may alter the potential for the soul to reach its cosmic consciousness. Should that occur, your Aquarius friend then becomes a professional student, a scientist, and a mental snob.

Aquarius, House Number 9

How does your Aquarius friend feel or behave in House Number 9? Look at House Number 9 in the Section Housing System and read the keywords and get more information. This is the area of religion, traveling, learning, teaching, publishing and relationships with foreigners. In this area, your male or female Aquarius friend becomes a sophisticated Libra. This sign rules the law, psychology and the more advanced science of Astropsychology. Libra is ruled by artistic Venus, or in Greek mythology "The Goddess of Love" and signifies why Aquarius is also a very creative sign. As Libra rules the balancing of energies, diplomacy, contracts and partners, your male or female friend born in February will always be concerned with what makes people the way they are. Aquarius' legendary curiosity and commitment to mankind is coming from the diplomatic oriented sign of Libra in this House of high studying. Venus, the ruler of this House, will always stimulate Aquarius' strong desire to understand others and bring about Universal Love and respect to all. In this Libra (peace oriented) House, many February souls are born crusaders for the justice of all, and must reach a firm balance in all of their scientific, or humanitarian endeavors. This attitude usually transforms the soul into a psychologist, Astropsychologist, attorney, or a counselor of some kind. The young Aquarius soul may also become a preacher for a specific revolutionary, or organized religious group. The advanced Aquarian is aware of the importance of keeping the balance of nature intact and will work endlessly to educate the world. Libra or the sign of commitment and marriage rules this House. Thus, in the 9th House of foreign affairs, many souls born in February end up marrying a foreigner (as I did), or operate and live (as I do) in a foreign land.

Aquarius, House Number 10

Let's now get into House Number 10. This is the area of career, public standing, and accomplishments. In this House your male or female Aquarius friend becomes a very powerful and mystical Scorpio. Refer to the Section Housing System and read more to understand this House or this Sign better. Pluto, "The Lord of Hades" in Greek mythology, rules Scorpio. Thus, your male or female Aquarius friend has been given the opportunity to explore sex, power, metaphysics, the medical field, high science, corporate money and establish a very powerful if not dramatic career. Scorpio rules also life and death, the police force, the mafia, investigations, night and secretive endeavors. The advanced Aquarius soul has much spiritual regeneration to offer the world and will strive in rebirthing people, physically or spiritually. The sign of Scorpio rules ultimate power and death while Aquarius rules freedom and shocking surprises. President Ronald Reagan's assassination attempt is a good example of an Aquarius' dramatic career and his position before the public. The same Scorpio energy is at work with police officers as they face the criminals of our society. Thus, they submit their precious lives in the face of danger, as they serve to protect the public. Due to Scorpio's dramatic impact in this particular House, the young February soul may easily fall for a less glamorous, sexual, or criminal career, and in the process solicit an early death. Your male or female Aquarius friend will attract any career demanding secret endeavors, investigation, danger, sex and passion. The best career description for an Aquarius would be to become a "007-secret agent" where danger, passion, and sex rules the dramatic life of the subject. Incidentally, for specific karmic purposes, the young soul of your female Aquarius friend has been born extremely magnetic and incredibly beautiful. Some born in February may be involved with night work where the night Lizard or poisonous Scorpio stinger thrives on sex, money, manipulation, and power in their chosen career. The dark purpose is to bring about the lowest, animalistic instinct in man and invite destructive karma for all parties involved. The advanced Aquarius soul inherited much more power at birth, and tends to use it wisely to bring about the Eagle or the best in an individual's life.

Aquarius, House Number 11

How does your male or female friend born in February feel about friends? Let's simply look in House Number 11, and for more information look in the Section Housing System. This is the area of wishes, friends and group organizations. In this House Aquarius becomes a spiritual Sagittarius. Jupiter or "The Lord of Luck" in Greek mythology rules the sign of Sagittarius. Knowing that Sagittarius rules foreign lands, your male or female friends born in February will not be short of friends from all over the world. Aquarius loves to communicate via telephone with friends who are far away, and those who are not so far away. Sagittarius rules also publishing, teaching, traveling; and your male or female friend born in February has a strong wish for education and writing. Sometimes the advanced Aquarius soul will involve a close friend in their publishing business ventures. In this case, my beautiful Cancer friend, Melquida (from Verona — e-mail address: scubadeedo@hotmail.com), is the editor of this work; thereby, reflecting how the stars work in the lives of friends and people. This House rules also wishes, and your Aquarius friend has a serious desire to travel, visit foreign lands, to learn, and to teach others. Many wishes of your male or female friends born in February will be offered by foreigners or by operating in a foreign land. For business or pleasure, they often do travel with a friend who is a foreigner. Sagittarius is intellectually and spiritually inclined; thus, your male or female Aquarius friend will be attracted to this type of friend in their life. Being so magnetic and original, your male or female Aquarius friend will also demand understanding and freedom from their friends. An Aquarius is warm, direct, loving, caring, and will feel really sad losing your friendship. Friends do bring them all their wishes and very often love is introduced to them this way. Your male or female friend born in February will travel far and fast to find the true spiritual friend and lover they are so desperately looking for. They usually succeed, sometimes later in life.

Aquarius, House Number 12

Let's now investigate what is going on in the subconscious area of your male or female friend born in February. Look at House Number 12 in the Section Housing System for more information. This is the area of fear, imagination, the subconscious, hidden enemies, and deception. In this House, Aquarius becomes a precise Capricorn engineer. The subconscious motivation of your male or female friend born in February is to bring rationalization or science to one of the most illusive areas of the human experience, the subconscious. Thus, it is important for those born in February to understand what it means to be human and what it is that makes each one of us so unique. They need to uncover this secret so they can provide concrete help for their family and all the people they so deeply care for. Souls born in February were born to explore, understand and promote the intangible. Many souls born in February will spend time alone pondering the mystery of life, and what can be done to improve the purpose of mankind. Thus, many young Aquarius souls are inventors, astronomers, psychologists, chemists, astrophysists, and explore a myriad of scientific topics. The advanced souls realize not only the physical aspects of life but are also able to dwell with the intuitive values of the Universal Mind through their powerful subconscious. Many souls born in February are much too advanced for a slow-to-learn rational society, and spend much of their time investigating the unknown. They do strive for the spiritual professions, especially Astrology and Astropsychology; where they can appreciate the true meaning of what it means to be human by helping others psychically. Aquarius' inner motivation is to gather information and structure the subconscious so that in the future, the world will become a much better, and safer, place for all.

Astropsychology Profile
Pisces

Neptune (Poseidon) in Greek mythology rules souls born in the month of March. Theirs is the conventional Sun Sign of "the Fish." Neptune will give your Pisces friends the opportunity to swim upstream towards the light and true knowledge, and away from the dogmas. Pisces is also a karmic sign and may experience its last life on this dense physical world.

Pisces, House Number 1

The soul's purpose of your friends born in March is to find and accept spiritual reality, and then teach it to the rest of the world. Practical and caring, the advanced Pisces soul will swim upstream towards the Universal Mind and the stars

I Know All About You 201

where the soul came from. Find House Number 1 in the Section Housing System and read the keywords to get more information. The negative aspect of this sign is to only accept dogmatic religious material and impose its rigorous rules to others. Young souls born in March may also fall for the negative pull of Neptune and slowly sink into a world of deception, guilt, alcohol, drugs and frustration. March souls are very karmic by nature and must work much harder than any other Sun Sign to fight the worse energy of all, deceiving Neptune. Thus, they can also be fault finding, critical, extremely stubborn and reject all that does not fit their religious upbringing and idiosyncrasy. The advanced Pisces soul is extremely old and has more than the needed tools to handle the many dangers and deceiving traps along the way. This sign is a "terminal" of, and has been through so many past lives. Pisces is a reflection of all the signs of the zodiac, and it has retained in itself all prior lessons learned. The weakest sign of the zodiac can also be the strongest if chosen. Your male or female friend born in March is extremely sensitive and very creative, thus, teaching and healing appeal to them. Pisces is the sign in opposition to Virgo, the "Virgin Mary" or the symbol subconsciously chosen by Christianity. Thus, Pisces must swim upstream towards "The Virgin Mary" using critical thinking and practicality in all they do, and in their research for the truth. The strong pull of the Virgo Sun Sign can be used for organization, health, and paperwork; also it can be used to produce a very pious person with the puritanical virgin's desire for chastity.

Pisces, House Number 2

How does your friend born in March deal with money? In this money House, Pisces becomes an aggressive Aries. Look at House Number 2 in the Section Housing System, and read the keywords to get more information on both this sign and its respective House. Mars (The Lord of Fire and War) rules the sign of Aries; thus, some Pisces' will work in the fields of engineering, construction or where action, danger, fire, and competition are required. Neptune (The Lord of the Seas) rules Pisces. You will also find other Pisces' operating in the Navy, Army or in the oil industry. More creative and famous souls like Jerry Lewis, Quincy Jones and Ursula Andress, to name a few, will offer their artistic gifts to the world. Others simply become precise teachers to children. Aries rules the finding of the self and making good use of any talent. Once this is accomplished, your male or female friend born in March will become a leader in its chosen field and make tons of money in the process. You will find the Pisces loving and caring heart almost anywhere in the world where danger, dedication, self-sacrifice and spiritual health is needed. A quiet home or office is desperately needed for a soft Pisces to operate, especially if research, health, or communication is involved. The intuition, care and psychic ability they were born with is the perfect gift needed to perform, talk and guide the people around them. Because Neptune rules also the arts and psychic work, your male or female friends born in March will find themselves attracted or involved in those endeavors. They are adept at finding the right spiritual words to heal the most wounded souls walking this earth, and many advanced Pisces are very successful in their career endeavors. On a negative aspect, the young Pisces soul lacks stamina or discipline to establish his position in the world and aims for escapism via drugs or alcohol. Born into the water element, understanding and following the Moon's fluctuations or mastering Astropsychology would prove to be beneficial for them and the world at large. The planet Mars rules this House of money and self-esteem; and the desire to succeed is quite strong and usually reached. Spiritually or physically, all Pisces' possess an artistic touch.

Pisces, House Number 3

In their 3rd House, ruling the thinking process, your friends born in March become a stubborn Taurus. Look at House Number 3 in the Section Housing System and read the keywords to gather more information. Seeing life through rose colored glasses, the earthy and security-oriented sign of Taurus gives your dreamy Pisces friend the intellectual tools needed to be more rational. It also gives them the ability to deal with this dense physical world in a practical manner. The power of creative Venus (ruler of Taurus) will also give them a myriad of artistic talents via music, painting, drawing, acting, etc. On a negative note, the legendary Taurus laziness or indulgence with all that life has to offer will show on Pisces' physical appearance; thus, Pisces is strongly advised to get off the couch and to exercise. The mind of your male or female friend born in March is concerned mostly with money, security, and the arts. This mental attitude gives them the power for practical actions in all endeavors. However, the Bull is also very stubborn, and once your Pisces friend has made his mind up, it will be really hard if not impossible for them to change it. Also, regardless of age, the younger and more immature Pisces soul may be reluctant to change their religious views or faith once certain beliefs have been established. Remember that Taurus rules money; as a result, any mental exploration will bring about a relief, and monetary gain for the soul. The young soul who keeps resisting growth will make money with dogmatic teachings through this communication House. Many Pisces evangelists or priests are "spiritual leaders" in organized religions. The advanced Pisces soul, however, teaches God's highest truth as found in the creation of the Universal Mind via the light or the stars. Thus, your male or female friend born in March inherited a stubborn mind and must realize Taurus' traditional or conventional thinking process. Once the fear to expand is eliminated, the thought process becomes very powerful. This then allows Pisces to find and teach all of those who are in need of his unfailing spiritual guidance.

Pisces, House Number 4

Let's investigate House Number 4 for those born in March. Look at House Number 4 in the Section Housing System and read the keywords to get more information. In the home and family area, your male or female Pisces friend becomes a witty Gemini. A tiny planet called Mercury "The Messenger of The Gods" rules this sign. Gemini rules communication, photography, mental curiosity and this sign is continuously in constant motion. In that respect many Pisceans (like a "fish" in the ocean) will prefer to be and/or live on the move, on the road, in a boat. Others would rather reside in an exotic place close to the ocean. Pisces can also do well in a big city, but their home must also be an office with lots of books. The advanced Pisces will use their incredible imagination to produce great books or write beautiful music or poetry. Other Pisces' will regenerate at home with photography, painting or performing spiritual work via the telephone. Gemini means communication and brothers and sisters, thus your friend born in March needs to communicate with all the family members. Gemini is a double sign, and many Pisces souls have two residences, one by the water and the other high in the mountains where they hide away from the excessive demand and stress of the physical world. Like Virgo, Gemini, is a Mercury ruled sign, thus, mental stimulation and creativity from the base of operation is a must. The desire to exteriorize and explore is produced by Gemini's endless curiosity, and Pisces will find its way out through the use of computers and write or travel the world via the Internet. Many Pisces were raised in a city or semi-rural area, and very close to nature. The desire to re-establish nature around them is also quite strong. It is important for any Pisces to become creative at home as the swift planet Mercury will make them active and high-strung. Your male or female Pisces friend is also prone to purchase properties with a brother or a sister. Much of the daily activities or stress will be shared with the family. This is all fine as long as the complaining aspect of the Fish is not exaggerated to the point of becoming a burden to others. Gemini rules birds and talkative animals; many Pisces tend to surround themselves and work also with exotic animals.

Pisces, House Number 5

Let's move on to the 5th House of love and romance and see how your male or female friend born in March becomes when dealing with love. Investigate House Number 5 in the Section Housing System and read the keywords. In this House, your Pisces friend turns into an emotional and sensitive Cancer. Thus, Pisces will attract other water signs such as Cancer, Scorpio or an earth sign such as Virgo. Like all water signs Pisces strives for emotion and security; this is usually found with well-established people they are attracted to. Pisces are often extraordinary sensitive and totally unselfish with those they care for. In matters of love no other sign can offer such a commitment of caring. Because of this altruistic attitude many souls born in March must not get involved with anyone just for the sake of having a relationship. Beauty of the heart is more important to them than mere physical attraction and they need total emotional commitment from you. They are looking at you as someone who needs to be cherished and protected at all costs and this motherly attitude may not necessarily fit a more independent or intellectual sign. Cancer rules food, security and all family matters, thus power, status and accomplishments serve only as a mean of security and are of secondary importance. They need to know that their chosen partner needs them at all times. Once a partner has been picked, your male or female friend born in March will face all challenges and will never stop loving you. They are capable of incredible sacrifices and will find it hard to let go of the past. Pisces rules self sacrifice while Cancer rules children. Many Pisces do extremely well with children and are very aware of their needs. In that respect not many people will match their standards for love and attention. This House rules also speculation. It is important for them to respect the Moon's fluctuations in all affairs controlled by this House. The awareness and respect of the Universal Laws can only propel a Pisces to the highest level of accomplishment. Note that Albert Einstein, born March 14, 1879 was additionally born with his Dragon's Head in Aquarius; see ***The Power of the Dragon.*** On the negative aspect, the young Pisces soul will be insecure and shy and could destructively manipulate the emotions of their lover. The advanced soul takes on the challenges imposed by Neptune who ultimately rewards them with true accomplishment and true love.

Pisces, House Number 6

In the 6th House of work health and service, a soul born in March becomes a powerful Leo. Investigate House Number 6 in the Section Housing System for the keywords. This zodiac sign rules love, life, art, fame, children and all that means the light of the Sun itself. Thus, any profession where light and life can be offered to others including health, is something that will appeal to a Pisces. Thus, your male or female friend born in March was born an artist and has the potential for great fame. Such famous Pisces people such, as Alan Thicke, Vanessa Williams, Quincy Jones and Ursula Andress are accomplished actors and humanitarian at heart. The strong Pisces emotional and acting sense makes for great actors and singers. Your male or female friend born in March is naturally looking for the sunlight and many of them work well with the stars and will further homeopathic medicine. Because Pisces is a self-sacrificing sign, a strong creativity and a refined sense of care is often displayed in their chosen career. This sign is altruistic in nature but at work, the soft and shy Pisces becomes a powerful Leo. The young soul may become self-centered and display an obvious spiritual pride. While the advanced true Pisces soul will exhibit a legitimate caring attitude with co-workers. A glamorous and artistic environment at work is a must for those born in March. Many Pisces works as music or dance teachers where they do stand on stage in front of the children they care so much for. Under stress Pisces may develop insomnia and guilt and could complain constantly making it miserable for others. Pisces rules the subconscious, and souls born in March must feel that he or she is a part of an important purpose that will alleviate the physical or spiritual suffering of mankind. This water sign is extremely creative and loves any challenge were creativity and originality is concerned. Many souls born in March will travel far to pass on their powerful message. Some will chose to service the world using the creative force of the Sun to reach fame as a nurse, an artist, or a teacher. Leo rules the heart and the true Pisces inner drive will allow many souls born in March to fulfill their deep need to alleviate the suffering of mankind.

Pisces, House Number 7

So now let's look in the House of marriage and see how those born in March deal with the world. In the 7th House of relationships, your male or female Pisces friend becomes a critical Virgo. Investigate House Number 7 in the Section Housing System for the keywords. Because Virgo is a perfectionist in so many ways, many Pisces will attract organized and health oriented partners. Virgo is an earth sign and has quite a lot of interest in health matters; thus, the chosen partner must be practical and healthy in many different ways. Geared by criticism, March souls could easily become extremely critical with the world and with their partner; and in the process seriously damage their existing relationship. Mercury, the ruler of Virgo rules communication, learning, and teaching. Thus, they could also attract this type of partnership. Virgo rules the 6th House of work and in the 7th House of marriage, many souls born in March will work hard to preserve their relationships. The marriage partner is usually found or met on the working environment. The young Pisces soul could also attract a Virginal, rigid or religious partner and may even join them in the deep deceptive waters of Neptune. Your male or female friend born in March will demand total honesty and purity in any relationship. The critical

Virgo attitude makes them shy and picky and could slow down the process of finding a good mate. To make things worse, the cold Virgo nature may make them feel much too good or much too pure for any true relationship and the young soul turns itself into a nun or a priest serving a deity. On a more positive note, the advanced Pisces soul has no problem offering his true Virginal love and sacrifice to his respectful partner. There is no limit to how high and rewarding, the positive fish swimming upstream, can offer a partner in life. Turning into a health oriented, perfectionist Virgo in facing the world, many Pisces' are attracted to a medical career. Facing the world as a critical Virgo your advanced or less advanced male or female friend born in March could lead himself in one of the following endeavors: a herbalist, editor, fashion designer, physician, teacher, speaker, cinematography, photography or writing. Also, some Pisces' find the career as a psychic detective very rewarding.

Pisces, House Number 8

Lets see what's going on in House Number 8 for those born in March. In the area of life and death, legacy, metaphysics, sex and corporate money, your male or female Pisces friend becomes a diplomatic Libra. Look at House Number 8 in the Section Housing System for more keywords. Libra rules the law and justice while this House rules affairs of the dead. Thus, many souls born in March are quite concerned with what will happen to those they care for after their demise. Sharing equally their possessions with those they love is important to them and many thoughts will be geared in that direction. Libra rules the kidneys, thus, in order to avoid serious health problems, souls born in March must not put stress or abuse on that organ. Thus, Pisces is strongly advised not to overindulge themselves with alcohol or any chemicals. This House rules insurance and many Pisces' will receive financial settlements in their lifetime. Or in the case of them being homeless, help will come from a legal endeavor to dispose of the body. Libra is an artistic sign giving those born in March the opportunity to make quite a lot of money through contracts. Souls born in March have a great potential to build long lasting financial securities using the psychological or Astropsychological values of this sign of Libra. Pisces has a true desire to help, and the potential to gain financial reward may come from working for a group while helping those in need. In the affairs of sex, a solid emotional commitment must be established otherwise there could be difficulties enjoying sex. This House rules also metaphysics, psychic work, investigation and the potential to make money not only with a group but also with a business or marriage partner. Pisces is not naturally super competitive but can and will find strength, and courage in working in or for a group. The more advanced souls born in March have great structuring potential and many works with large financial corporations. The 8th House involves corporate money and business resources; thus, Pisces has been given the potential to lead and seal all the elements involving the affairs of this particular House.

Pisces, House Number 9

How does your Pisces friend feel or behave in House Number 9? This is the area of religion, traveling, learning, teaching, publishing and relationships with foreigners. In this area your male or female Pisces friend becomes a very powerful Scorpio. Look at House Number 9 in the

Section Housing System and read the keywords to gather more information. Pluto (Lord of Life and Death and Transformation) rules Scorpio. Because Scorpio rules also metaphysics, high science and general investigation, any education on these topics will bring financial rewards and growth to Pisces. The soul must find himself with the transforming power of Pluto and use the creative forces of this planet to further true light to the world. Scorpio is naturally very intense and super emotional while this particular House rules also religion. Thus, many young souls born in March will become professional students of dogmatic teaching and will not be able to perceive or teach anything else than their religious values. This archaic attitude slows down true cosmic consciousness and transforms the soul into a preacher of dogmas, or a fanatical religious leader. The advanced Pisces soul knows better and will teach the highest truth found in the universal mind. As a rule, not many Pisces' miss the essence of the light of the stars and its jurisdictions over mankind for the holy printed word. Pisces does and will regenerate by studying, traveling and philosophizing; thereby undergoing a spiritual or religious metamorphosis. Through the deadly energy of the Scorpion, Pisces regenerates the Scorpion's deadly energy; Pisces, henceforth, undergoes a deep spiritual/religious metamorphosis. In this, he or she becomes a "reborn" Christian or embraces a new religion. Once the independent self and the celestial truth are reached, those born in March are given the opportunity by the stars to become leaders in this House of teaching and publishing. The advanced soul will reach the masses and will pass on his knowledge with care and without spiritual pride. Pisces is extremely sensitive, while Scorpio is only concerned with the truth regardless of the danger involved. Souls born in March will travel around the world, and many of them tend to meet with their death in foreign countries. Many famous and wealthy Pisceans will operate outside of their country of birth to help alleviate pain and suffering in the world. Many of the advanced ones spend much of their time teaching the world. This House rules traveling and teaching the masses at large, it also rules the Indians, and animals.

Pisces, House Number 10

Let's now get into House Number 10. This is the area of career, public standing and accomplishments. In this area your male or female Pisces friend becomes a very spiritual Sagittarius. Look at House Number 10 in the Section Housing System and read the keywords to get more information. Remember you can also refer to the Sun Sign Characteristics and read all about this Sun Sign. Jupiter or "The Lord of the Lords" in Greek mythology rules Sagittarius. Thus, your male or female Pisces friend has been given the opportunity to travel around the world and become a leader in the spiritual or artistic fields. Jupiter rules also traveling, foreigners, animals, teaching, foreign lands, and the codification of thoughts, meaning the law or religion. Thus, Pisces is attracted to education and many turn themselves into caretakers, doctors, attorneys, teachers, philosophers, religious leaders, or even refined artists. Chances are that your Pisces friend will spend time for a good cause and will never cover his back if you are in need. In the medical aspect of astrology, Pisces rules the feet and accidents are prone on the ankles or in the water. Souls born in March are fully aware of the needs of others and will do all they can and more to help the needy. Your male or female friend born in March can also become a doormat and refuse the harsh realities of life. This negative attitude could also bring drug or alcohol abuse to help forget the painful reality. Pisces rules the spirit and the subconscious while Sagittarius in the 10th House rules career, and philosophy. The world can only recognize the potential, the caring attitude and the intellectual value of anyone born in March. Traveling the world to teach the truth to others is a remarkable mission to fulfill, and Pisces was born to do just that, and to do it very well.

Pisces, House Number 11

How does your male or female friend born in March feel about friends? This is the area of wishes, friends and group organization. In this area a Pisces becomes a practical Capricorn. Look at House Number 11 in the Section Housing System and read the keywords to get more information. You may also refer to the Sun Sign characteristics and read all about Capricorn. Saturn "The Great Malefic" rules this House and the sign of Capricorn. Knowing that Capricorn rules social standing, career and accomplishments, your male or female friend born in March will surely attract well-established friends. This is also the House of wishes, thus, many of Pisces' friends will provide practical help to them. In exchange Pisces will offer his tremendous spiritual guidance and total commitment. Because Pisces can sense his own business limitation or stamina to succeed he may chose to involve a close friend in a business venture. Capricorn is the sign of structure and power, thus, in this particular House, your dreamy Pisces friend becomes practical. The young religious Pisces soul could also use and abuse a wealthy friend's position to gather the financial support and reach a position of authority. Capricorn loves uptown gatherings and will, as a close friend, invite his Pisces friend to mingle with money, power and local authorities. The advanced fish is aware of the blessings from his friends, and will only uses the contacts and opportunities he received to further a true and honest purpose. Thus, both parties will benefit from each other's friendship for the common good of all. This House rules also groups and wishes and as a Capricorn, your Pisces friend has a serious desire to become a figure of authority within a spiritual or less spiritual group. This is indeed a full representation of the power (Saturn) and manipulation (Neptune) found in organized (Capricorn) religion (Pisces). Capricorn is not an emotional sign, thus, your male or female Pisces friend will be reluctant to build a close relationship with those who will not help him succeed on the ladder of success. However, once the goal is reached, the soft Pisces nature usually takes over and the friends are warmly loved and respected. In this wishes and friends House Pisces is well aware of the rat race and of their own limitations to reach the top. Thus, the Capricorn structuring power is used constructively with friends. Friends born in January, November and July will be attracted to Pisces and many will help them reach their dream for a better world. In return for the practical help received, deep feelings and true caring will be offered unselfishly.

Pisces, House Number 12

Lets now investigate the subconscious area of your male or female friend born in March. This is the area of fear, imagination, the subconscious and deception and ruled by Pisces. In this area your Pisces friend becomes a futuristic Aquarius. Investigate House Number 12 in the Section Housing System and read the keywords to get more information. Pisces is a very spiritual sign and loves to spend time in its own world of imagination. While in the subconscious area, the Aquarius' power will want him to see and imagine the future of mankind. Thus, it is important for those born in March to get away from it all and let their powerful imagination take over the harsh realities of life. Because Aquarius rules astrology, the advanced Pisces soul is naturally gifted to master the secret of the universal mind and perceive the future. In that respect, many famous psychics were born with both a strong Pisces or Aquarius in their chart. The less evolved Pisces will refuse to grow within the universal scheme of things and may invite madness through a constant study or teaching of the apocalyptic religious poisoning. Pisces rules the hidden part of the human psyche and souls born in March are prone to much subconscious fears and guilt. Neptune (Lord Of Deception) rules this House and the sign of Pisces making it even more difficult to let go of the past. Incidentally, Christians also chose the fish to represent their religion. Young souls born in March are very concerned with religious material and are unable to swim upstream and free themselves from the quicksand of illusory Neptune. Aquarius rules the future, originality, and freedom of thinking, universal love and group organization. Thus, your male or female friend born in March feels the importance to further the light he perceives as the truth to the rest of the world. It is important for those born in March to control their fear of not being able to reach the deep spiritual truth they are so desperately looking for to teach the world. They must understand that Aquarius rules not only their subconscious, but also the future and the stars; while Pisces is reluctant to expand outside of religious doctrines. The subconscious conflict is real but can be overcome by exploring externally in building a strong and practical cosmic consciousness. As its last life on this dense physical world, the advanced Pisces soul will learn all the secrets of the Aquarius Universal Mind and finally break the reincarnation principle. Hence, Pisces then becomes a co-creator with himself and with God.

Responses from my readers

Many people out there have investigated my **Moon Power** books. Their e-mail, letters and telephone comments are pouring in non-stop. The feedback experienced on my radio show produces phenomenal responses. Here is some responses from some of those wise people.

Dr. Turi, you are truly AMAZING! I did not miss that in my 99 Starguide, or any of the other "right on" predictions... After your course Dr. Turi, it is easy to identify people's signs pretty much, I am so tuned to what I thought were habits but it is their placed planets that give them these qualities. Dr. Turi I placed a call last week to you or Heather about an order of some more 99 Starguide and forecasts to see if they had been shipped, I believe I sent for them Jan 22nd, could you see if these are "in the mail", my friends love them, so I keep purchasing them...they are the best gifts anyone can give their friends.... Thank you Again and again! Good energies to you...../// A. //Eb///

Dear Dr. Turi:
Since being instructed by you on the positive & negative cycles of the moon I have endeavored to adjust my lifestyle to accommodate what I have learned. Case in point, Six

years ago a drunk driver smashed into my truck. Fortunately, no one was hurt, but my vehicle was totaled. Over the years I have taken him to court numerous times with no positive result. After all the time and expense of pursuing the case I was seriously considering discontinuing my efforts to collect my court judgment. However, after learning the Universal Law I sent the defendant a diplomatic letter at the beginning of the new moon suggesting a new plan for payment. The incredible than happened, he called me. Keep in mind that this man dodged me for 6 long years, and I had since moved out of the state where the accident occurred. Thanking me for my time and patience, he assured me that payment would shortly follow and it did, in one lump sum. Needless to say, I am very happy especially since the dollar amount was in the thousands. I am convinced that utilizing the moon cycle was a contributing factor to putting this matter to bed. This is good stuff.
Sincerely, Kenn ///berg
P.S You may use this for a testimonial if you so desire.

Subject: From one of your students
Dear Dr. Turi:
God bless you – I love your *1999 Moon Power* – it is well written and gives more info than the 1998 version. I am learning so much about life and love I thank you again from the bottom of my heart. And even my sons whose readings you did are starting to ask me what planets are in control.
Your friend, Ellen ///ow

From your student
Dear Dr. Turi
Definitely Divine Astrology for me, I have never been

exposed to any Astrology before hearing Dr. Turi on Jeff Rense's national program, but if modern Astrology is littered with mathematical jargon then it is more of a hand down Win for Divine Astrology. The favorite part for me was Dr. Turi's great humor through out the tapes, I of course need to practice the reflex and know it will get more interesting when I receive my computer program and plug in people I know birth dates to practice with the housing system.
Thank you, Joyce

To: dr.turi@juno.com (Louis Turi) Date: Thu, 04 Feb 1999 18:47:55 -0800 Subject: Reading - Hello Dr. Turi, Michele ////r here — I received your tape-reading today — and was thrilled! It was a positive reading (basically the bad stuff is over and the good stuff is coming). I know you get tons of mail and may not specifically remember my reading, or me but (DOB 8/13/59) the Egyptian Cross cards were (1) the Sun, (2) death, (3) the judge/king and (4) the wheel of fortune. You seemed excited and pleased and suggested that as soon as I could I should———

From: "@marsweb.com
Hi Dr. Turi;
My name is Karen ///. My friend Zarah /// wrote you an e-mail earlier today. I thought I would write a quick note to introduce myself. I live in Choteau, MT. When I lived in WA in May of 97 I taped your interview on 'Sightings'. I felt an instant soul connection with you. And I was thrilled hearing that you came home after your trip with our star brothers and painted emblems on your house. I know that you are doing a great work and would love to meet you in person some day.

I Know All About You

From: ///n9@aol.com
Hello Dr. Turi,
I just wanted you to know what a great reading you gave me. The tarot was right on the mark! I am changing my career and was glad to find out about the great opportunities ahead. I have always been around assholes. I know I am on the right road and it just feels great. The astrology part will help me be based as to what I am and how to go about. I got the greatest energy from hearing all of it.
In the Light, Nancy ////e

From: ////@dewittec.net
Hi Dr. Turi,
A gentleman asked about you so I sent him over to the "Predictions" page. His response is below, followed by a subsequent response. Have a very good one, Jocelyn.

Closing Thoughts

Today's date is May 7th, 2000

Dear Clients and Friends:

I would like to sincerely thank you for your patronage and wish all of you a very successful New Year. It has been my privilege, with **"I Know All About You!"** to bring more cosmic consciousness in your life. Do you need any of my services or do you have a product or a service to offer my large clientele worldwide? If so visit http://drturi.com or call the offices at 619-275-5853 or write to Dr. Louis Turi: PO Box 81529 San Diego, CA 92138. You may also get more info on my services, videos and download my books at http://drturi.com. Being at the right place at the right time has a lot to do with your progress in terms of opportunities. My work will be a major contribution to your success in your life.

Also, please help me promote the cosmic consciousness of everyone you care about. I need both your spiritual and financial help to build many Astropsychology schools for the children of tomorrow. Understand the importance of my mission and be a part of it in the unfolding world karma. Please help me and invest in the future in promoting the true knowledge of the stars. Your contributions will help me so that I can spend more time on the air, writing, educating and publishing my work to those in need. For centuries much resources have been wasted to discredit the stars and in wasteful and dangerous religious dogmas. Times have changed and the stars above do impose a new consciousness for mankind. Be a promoter of light and invest in the true light. The children of tomorrow need to gain cosmic consciousness and use the stars to live a more productive and safe life. Please communicate my work and help those in need to find guidance, comfort, direction and assistance in the celestial order. I hope you will find in "I Know All About You" the pathway to the stars and the realization of God's ultimate will throughout the Universe.

Walk in peace with your new knowledge of the stars

God bless you all

– Dr. Turi

He is wise who understands that the stars are luminaries, created as signs. He who conquers the stars will hold the golden keys to God's mysterious universe.

– Nostradamus

New Cover for revised "Power of The Dragon"
About the cover Illustrator

I am Madeline Rosenstein and I majored in art and received my Bachelor of Arts from the University of California – Berkeley. I then went onto San Diego State University where I studied printmaking, and received my Master's Degree. I then taught art at the college level for a few years until branching out into various graphic arts projects (i.e., sign painting, logo design and illustrations). I have had the pleasure of teaching art classes to young school children, as well as working for an Oregon winery designing their wine labels and silk-screening their gift boxes.

I am thankful to Dr. Turi. As not knowing my educational background in art he conducted an Astropsy-chology reading for me that was "right on the money." (Pardon the pun.) He defined my calling as an artist without even knowing that I was one!

Dr. Turi went on to explain that I was born with the Dragon's Head in Pisces, and that other planets like Jupiter and Mercury were there too; and that the planets Venus and the Sun were in Capricorn. Wow!!

To-date I am moving forward with my artwork, and am very happy. I am currently creating a series of posters of the 12 signs of the zodiac.

Again, I am graciously thankful for Dr. Turi's Astropsychology reading. It honestly has given me the tools and meaning to look deeper into my own work and share my soul's gift, with others.

Please visit me on my website at: www.madroseart.com

or write me at :
Madeline Rosenstein
4130 SW 117th Avenue, #298
Beaverton, OR 97005-8999.
E-mail address: madroseart@hotmail.com

And now you know "ALL ABOUT ME!"

Startheme Ltd.

Financial Investment Guidance & Investigative Astropsychology

Post Office Box 81529
San Diego CA 92138-1529
(619) 275-5853
http://drturi.com

"Millionaires don't use Astrology, billionaires do!"
— J.P. Morgan

Just because you cannot see it or read it does not mean it doesn't exist. Large businesses and corporations are missing out on vital information not available in books or business courses.

These same corporations will rise and ultimately collapse, because they omitted this pertinent information. This lack of awareness can jeopardize your finances, career, security and stocks.

Do you know that you can get fluctuations of the stock market months ahead of time? How would you like to know the right time and the right area for your investments? How would you like to know all about your financial business partners or your employees true values? Would you like to know which business associates to work with or the best employee's to hire? If you are a company owner, C.E.O., a President or investor of a large corporation, be aware that there is no room for ignorance and your competition might already be my client.

Call Dr. Turi for a private consultation at 1-800-640-0025 Extension 13

> **Dr. Turi Regular Radio Programs:**
> **Dr. Turi** and **Jeff Rense** — **Live Coast-to-Coast**
> Every 3rd Thursday of every month.
> Worldwide on the Internet via RealAudio
> Visit <www.sightings.com>

Dear Client and Friend,

As you know prices are skyrocketing everywhere on everything. However, you will benefit from a very special offer — only $200.00 per reading (regularly $497.00 Full Life Reading) which lasts about 60 minutes. Visit his site at **http://drturi.com/** for more information about Dr. Turi's services, your daily or weekly forecast and his weekly newsletter. You may also send your request and payment to: **Dr. Turi, P.O. Box 81529, San Diego, CA 92138-1529.**

Product Ordering

We offer four easy ways to order:

The first and fastest way to order is **directly on-line** with our Secure Server. When ordering books using the order form on our Secure Server, you will receive a link to the "eBook" version of the paperback which can be downloaded within 10 minutes. If you order using one of our other methods the eBook will be emailed to you within 72 hours. All other books, videos and course orders will be shipped within 24 hours. All personal readings will be handled directly by Dr. Turi and will be shipped within 7 to 10 business days.

The second method, is downloade our **printable version** of the order form. Print it, fill it in and then this can be faxed to: (619) 275-4416 or mailed to: Dr. Turi, P.O. Box 81529, San Diego, CA 92138-1529.

Or, you can use your credit card and order by phone, (619) 275-5853. When you order through the phone your eBook can still be emailed to you; but within 72 hours, not 10 minutes as with our on-line ordering. Also, for this option if you are ordering any of the personal readings you will need to have the date of birth, place of birth and the time of birth ready at the time you order. If you use this option please call during regular business hours, 9:00 AM to 6:00 PM Pacific Time.

The last way to order is through the mail. All you have to do is write your name, address, and the product and quantity of your order on a piece of paper. If you are ordering any of the personal readings, you will also need to include; the date of birth, place of birth and time of birth, and send it, along with your payment plus shipping and handling to: Dr. Turi, P.O. Box 81529, San Diego, CA 92138-1529.

All North American orders will be shipped using the United States Postal system. International shipping orders will incur extra costs. An invoice via email will be sent.

If you decide to use our fastest method, our on-line Secure Server, you can select the quantity of each item and then add it to your shopping cart. You will then be sent to the shopping cart section each time to double check what you have ordered and the quantity. Once there. you can choose to pay now or continue shopping. If you choose to pay now you will then be asked for your personal information including: name, shipping address, credit card number and expiration, date of birth, place of birth and time of birth. Once you have successfully completed this form and submitted it you will receive a thank you note and order confirmation via autorepsonder. This will let you know that your order has been received and is being processed.

Again, if you are are downloading an eBook, you will receive confirmation immediately and your order will be received within 10 minutes. If you are ordering books, videos, or courses your order will be shipped within 24 hours. All personal readings will be handled directly by Dr. Turi, and will be shipped within 7 to 10 business days.

From Promotional Director Startheme Publications LTD

Dr. Turi
Astrological Services
Readings
Visit http://drturi.com/

Full Life Reading:

A personalized detailed reading on a 2-60-minute audiotapes that will be used throughout your life. Simply unarguable facts about your direct relationship with the universal mind that will help you to establish emotional, financial and spiritual stability. A must for everybody! Progressive Reading: If you can not afford a Full Life Reading then a progressive reading is your next best choice. Like a Full Life reading, in a progressive reading I will explore and explain in great detail what is going on in the 12 specific areas of your life. I will translate the will of the cosmos as it is right now affecting your destiny, your financial situation, your love, your health, your career etc.Comparison Chart: Improve, save or find a quality business or emotional relationship with this service. Your stars have life and like an intriguing painting, colors blend harmoniously. Understand your partner's strengths and weaknesses for a more productive life.

Astro-Carto-Graphy:

Find the best place in the US and anywhere in the world where the stars above will offer you an easy reach to the best that life has to offer. Don't relocate without it. Children Characterology: Do not hesitate to invest in your child. You might have given life to a genius or an artist. Find out how and why your child thinks or behaves with you or the world at large.

Courses

Divine Astrology Course: Master Nostradamus' rare 16th Century method of Astrology rekindled as Astropsychology by Dr. Louis Turi. Nothing less than mind boggling to those searching for the truth.Celestial Dating Game: Learn in great detail the seat of attraction between human beings using Dr. Turi's revolutionary Astropsychology technique.

Appearences

Radio and Television Schedules and Bookings. What broadcasting professionals say about Dr. Turi's work. Links to Internet syndicated radio shows to hear Dr. Turi Live! Contact the Promotional Director Suzy Sands at Startheme Publications Ltd. to find out where and when Dr. Turi will be speaking.

Bookstores and Lectures

Schedules and Bookings. Contact the Promotional Director, Suzy Sands at Startheme Publications Ltd. to find out where and when Dr. Turi will be speaking.

Full Life Reading $497.95 —
See special offer page 222

This detailed reading will be used throughout your existence. I will explain (using Divine Astrology) the significance of all the planets in your horoscope and thoroughly clarify, all the vital departments of your life. In addition to adding new insight to your personality, this tape uncovers unique information based on the location of your natal Dragon's Head and Tail and the teaching of the implacable Universal Law. Keep in mind I do not practice the Astrology you know, read, practice or have studied. My work is totally unique and does not resemble any previous psychic readings or astrological work you may have experienced. All readings are taped on two top quality cassette tapes. All your questions will be answered and the right direction/guidance for a successful career or specific problem will be offered. The second part of your reading is the psychic cleansing and reading of your own Supraconscious forces in time and space. All areas of your future and past life residue will be covered.

NOTE: You do not have to be present for me to do your Full Life Reading. High quality 60-minute cassette tapes are used and sent daily all around the United States and the world. You may call the office at 619-275-5853 (evening please) for more information first!

Progressive Reading: $197.95

If you can not afford a Full Life Reading then a progressive reading is your next best choice. Like a Full Life reading, in a progressive reading I will explore and explain in great detail what is going on in the 12 specific areas of your life. I will translate the will of the cosmos as it is right now affecting your destiny, your financial situation, your love, your health, your career etc. I will explore some of your past lives residue and tell you how to make a good use of them, I will explain both the location of the Dragon's Head and Tail by House and sign so that you can make incredible progress almost immediately in any area of your life. I will look into the next two years ahead of you and do very specific prediction and even give you the exact months you can expect the changes to take place. I will do "The Egyptian Cross" astro-tarot reading towards the end of your 90 mn tape. This is a cleansing of your subconscious in time and space and neutralize the negative energy surrounding you. A progressive reading is a "must do" yearly tape that will guide and help you as the progressive or dramatic changes are taking place in your life.

Comparison Chart: $149.95 Per Person
Marriage / Business Comparison Relationships:

Improve, save or find a quality relationship with this service. Discover the differences between you and your partner and learn how to promote only the best of his/her stars. Understand how to promote the strengths and eliminate the weakness of the alliance. Realize what are the difficulties or opportunities you face together. While providing a thorough discussion of issues suggested by your charts, I will also give special attention to the fears, weaknesses and karmic residue of both. The location of your respective dragon, by sign and House can seriously promote or alter a relationship. Find out what to do or not to do financially or emotionally with that person, remember knowledge is power. Will his/her stars promote or disintegrate your life? Be aware, save time and money. This tape is a must for any marriage or business venture with a new partner.

Astro-Carto-Graphy — $149.95

Map your future. Don't relocate without it! Find out where and what the best of your stars have to offer you. You may be just a few hundred miles from a splendid Venus (love) Sun (fame) Jupiter (study) Mercury (writing) line. You might be, right now living and striving without any hope of success under a nefarious planet like Saturn (depression) or Neptune (drugs) or Mars (war). Take a chance for yourself and make your own reality, learn where those wonderful lines are waiting for you. Astrocartography really works! Back home in France I was under a nefarious Saturn line and the more I worked the less security or reward I had. Then I relocated under the Sun (fame) to California, in the US and anything that I touched turned out pure gold! The same goes for your home. Don't buy a house without checking it out, as you might not be able to keep it for long. Avoid financial stress (Saturn lines), avoid locations where you are prone to lose your home because nature devastative forces (Uranus lines). Avoid fires (Mars lines) instead let me explain those lines and guide you towards happiness (Jupiter) wealth (Venus) health power and fame (Sun). Call now for information, do not hesitate, your career and your house are your biggest and most important decision and investment you will have to make. Call me for info first — Dr. Turi (619) 275-5853. Work available by mail. World Wide Map, 25 pages of information tailored for you by Dr.Turi and a booklet will be also mailed to you.

Children's Characterology — $149.95

Find out why your child is the way he/she is. Give him/her the EARLY opportunity to regenerate his/her spirit and get the right direction in life. Let me introduce your star children, as you never knew them before. Do not let the worst of the stars take control over their destiny. In this day and age children need spiritual regeneration more than ever. The sad fact is that over 6000 of them commit suicide every year in the US alone while other children are killing each other in schools. Don't wait until itís too late, understand the dilemma from Astropsychology and let Dr. Turi help your child with this service. Your child's future is worth it! I saved many teenagers from suicidal tendencies, gang activity, drug/alcohol addictions and put them right back on track on the road of health, success and happiness. Save thousands of dollars on wasteful sessions of traditional psychotherapy and years of guilt and sorrow. Do it for his/her birthday and watch the results.

DR. TURI'S ORDER FORM

Qty.	Title	Price Each	Price

____ *Moon Power Starguide* eBook
Yearly Guidance & Predictions **$19.95** ____

____ *The Power of the Dragon* **$29.95** ____
Nostradamus Dragon Forecast For All Signs

____ (Yearly) eBook **$12.95** ____

____ *I know All About You* **$24.95** ____

____ *Reaching For The Light* **$29.95** ____
(in progress)

READINGS

____ *Taped Full Life Reading*
(2-60MN audio tape by mail/or in person)
Regularly $497.00 • Special **$200.00** ____

____ *Taped Progressive Reading* **$197.00** ____
(90MN audio tape by mail/or in person)

____ *Taped Comparison Chart* **$149.95** ____
(90MN audio tape by mail)

____ *Astro-Carto-Graphy* **$149.95** ____
(by mail with Dr. Turi's translation)

____ *Taped Child Characterology* **$149.95** ____
(60MN audio tape by mail)

COURSES

____ **Divine Astrology Course** **$997.00** ————
(16 Hour Course)

____ **Celestial Dating Game** **$497.00** ____
(8 Hour Course)

Sub-Total .... ____
Add $5.00 Shipping per Item .... ____

TOTAL .... ____

See Other Side – 2-sided form. Must fill-in other side also.

Necessary Processing Information – First Person

First Name _____ M.I.: _____
Last Name _____ _____
Address: _____
City _____ State _____ Zip: _____
Phone: (_____) _____-_____ E-Mail:_____ @ _____
D.O.B (month, day, year): _____ / _____ / _____ Ex: Feb. 26, 1950
Time of Birth: _____ : _____ AM or PM (Only for Astro-cartography)
Place of Birth: (City, State, Country): _____

Second Person Processing Information

First Name _____ M.I.: _____
Last Name _____ _____
Address: _____
City _____ State _____ Zip: _____
Phone: (_____) _____-_____ E-Mail:_____ @ _____
D.O.B (month, day, year): _____ / _____ / _____ Ex: Feb. 26, 1950
Time of Birth: _____ : _____ AM or PM (Only for Astro-cartography)
Place of Birth: (City, State, Country): _____

___ Check ___ Money Order ___ Credit Card

Credit Card # _____

Expiration Date _____ Type of Card: _____

Signature: _____

PRINT NAME AS ON CARD _____

DATE: _____ / _____ / _____

MAIL YOUR ORDER & PAYMENT PAYABLE TO:
Startheme Publications Ltd., P.O. Box 81529
San Diego, CA 92138-1529
Tel: (619) 275-5853 • Fax: (619) 275-4416
Knowledge is power - "ask and you shall receive"

DR. TURI'S ORDER FORM

Qty.	Title	Price Each	Price
____	*Moon Power Starguide* eBook Yearly Guidance & Predictions	$19.95	____
____	*The Power of the Dragon* Nostradamus Dragon Forecast For All Signs (Yearly) eBook	$29.95 $12.95	____
____	*I know All About You*	$24.95	____
____	*Reaching For The Light* (in progress)	$29.95	____

READINGS

____	*Taped Full Life Reading* (2-60MN audio tape by mail/or in person) *Regularly $497.00 • Special*	**$200.00**	____
____	*Taped Progressive Reading* (90MN audio tape by mail/or in person)	$197.00	____
____	*Taped Comparison Chart* (90MN audio tape by mail)	$149.95	____
____	*Astro-Carto-Graphy* (by mail with Dr. Turi's translation)	$149.95	____
____	*Taped Child Characterology* (60MN audio tape by mail)	$149.95	____

COURSES

____	**Divine Astrology Course** (16 Hour Course)	$997.00	_____
____	**Celestial Dating Game** (8 Hour Course)	$497.00	____
	Sub-Total		____
	Add $5.00 Shipping per Item		____
	TOTAL		____

See Other Side – 2-sided form. Must fill-in other side also.

Necessary Processing Information – First Person

First Name _____ M.I.: _____
Last Name ____ _____
Address: _____
City _____ State _____ Zip: _____
Phone: (_____) _____-_____ E-Mail:_____ @_____
D.O.B (month, day, year): _____ / _____ / _____ Ex: Feb. 26, 1950
Time of Birth: _____ : _____ AM or PM (Only for Astro-cartography)
Place of Birth: (City, State, Country): _____

Second Person Processing Information

First Name _____ M.I.: _____
Last Name ____ _____
Address: _____
City _____ State _____ Zip: _____
Phone: (_____) _____-_____ E-Mail:_____ @_____
D.O.B (month, day, year): _____ / _____ / _____ Ex: Feb. 26, 1950
Time of Birth: _____ : _____ AM or PM (Only for Astro-cartography)
Place of Birth: (City, State, Country): _____

___ Check ___ Money Order ___ Credit Card

Credit Card # _____

Expiration Date _____ Type of Card: _____

Signature: _____

PRINT NAME AS ON CARD _____

DATE: _____ / _____ / _____

MAIL YOUR ORDER & PAYMENT PAYABLE TO:
Startheme Publications Ltd., P.O. Box 81529
San Diego, CA 92138-1529
Tel: (619) 275-5853 • Fax: (619) 275-4416
Knowledge is power - "ask and you shall receive"

About Illustrator
The Front Cover
by Chris Tittle

Front cover painting and cover layout.

Chris Tittle is an artist and entrepreneur with a BFA in studio art from the University of New Mexico. He is President/CEO of CD Card Inc, a company specializing in the design and production of CD-ROM business cards and multimedia.

He is also owner and creative director of **Mantra Design**, the firm responsible for the design and maintenance of Dr. Turi's web site.

Check out CD Card Inc on the web at:
HYPERLINK
http://www.cdcard.ac

Check out Mantra Design on the web at:
HYPERLINK
http://www.mantradesign.com

Madeline Rosenstein — Back cover painting

www.ingramcontent.com/pod-product-compliance
Lightning Source LLC
Chambersburg PA
CBHW022056160426
43198CB00008B/255